PRAISE FOR

NEGOTIATING ARAB-ISRAELI PEACE
American Leadership in the Middle East

*"This rigorous, non-partisan, no-holds-barred analysis
of the most recent twenty years of U.S. effort in Middle
East peacemaking is essential reading for practitioners
and scholars. The operational implications have power-
ful potential in the hands of leaders who care about the
results as well as the politics of American statecraft in the
region."*

—Chester A. Crocker, the James R. Schlesinger
Professor of Strategic Studies, Georgetown University

*"I commend the authors of this book for their balanced
and critical analysis of the U.S. role in one of the most
pernicious conflicts of our time. The book publishes at a
critical juncture for U.S. leadership in the Middle East.
Its insights will be invaluable for many years to come."*

—Joschka Fischer, former foreign minister and vice
chancellor of Germany

*"*Negotiating Arab-Israeli Peace *is a tour de force that
deserves wide readership not only in the official, jour-
nalistic, and think tank worlds but also in academia.
This book should be widely utilized as a teaching tool
by professors who want to add real life practices to the
plethora of academic theory about conflict resolution and
peacemaking."*

—Samuel W. Lewis, former U.S. ambassador to
Israel and former director of the Policy Planning
Staff, U.S. Department of State

D0830552

"*Negotiating Arab-Israeli Peace comes at a pivotal moment for U.S. foreign policy. While delivering a critical assessment of the United States' mixed record in mitigating the conflict, this study reasserts America's crucial role in the Middle East peace process and provides a solid framework from which American policymakers and mediators can work to facilitate a comprehensive Arab-Israeli peace settlement.*"

—George J. Mitchell, former U.S. senator

"*This volume is the most forceful, thorough, concrete, and concise analysis of the U.S. performance in the Arab-Israeli peace process since it was born as a political process in 1974. The sharp call for energetic, determined, and disciplined perseverance in pursuit of the clear-cut U.S. interest in an Arab-Israeli-Palestinian peace sets the bar for our next president. It's a superb statement.*"

—Harold H. Saunders, former assistant secretary for Near Eastern and South Asian affairs, U.S. Department of State

"*In a direct and diplomatic analysis, this book dissects the past decades of U.S. inadequacies and outlines the requirements for an effective U.S. policy in the Middle East. It is the '1975 Brookings Report' of the next election, and it points sternly and creatively to the lessons and opportunities that we will be criminal to ignore. The United States Institute of Peace has done the nation a service in sponsoring the project, and the authors and their team have done the world a favor in looking so clearly into the past and the future.*"

—I. William Zartman, the Jacob Blaustein Professor of International Organizations and Conflict Resolution, Johns Hopkins University–SAIS

NEGOTIATING ARAB-ISRAELI PEACE

NEGOTIATING ARAB-ISRAELI PEACE

American Leadership in the Middle East

Daniel C. Kurtzer

Scott B. Lasensky

with
William B. Quandt, Steven L. Spiegel,
and Shibley I. Telhami

United States Institute of Peace Press
Washington, D.C.

The views expressed in this book are those of the authors alone. They do not reflect views of the United States Institute of Peace or any person interviewed or consulted by the study group.

United States Institute of Peace
1200 17th Street NW, Suite 200
Washington, DC 20036-3011
www.usip.org

© 2008 by the Endowment of the United States Institute of Peace. All rights reserved.

First published 2008

To request permission to photocopy or reprint materials for course use, contact Copyright Clearance Center at www.copyright.com.

Printed in the United States of America

The paper used in this publication meets the minimum requirements of American National Standards for Information Science—Permanence of Paper for Printed Library Materials, ANSI Z39.48-1984.

Library of Congress Cataloging-in-Publication Data

Kurtzer, Daniel.
    Negotiating Arab-Israeli peace : American leadership in the Middle East / Daniel Kurtzer, Scott Lasensky.
        p. cm.
    Includes bibliographical references and index.
    ISBN 978-1-60127-030-6 (pbk. : alk. paper)
 1. Arab-Israeli conflict--1993---Peace. 2. Israel--Politics and government--1993- I. Lasensky, Scott. II. United States Institute of Peace. III. Title.
 DS119.76.K87 2007
 956.05--dc22

                                    2007044149

Contents

FOREWORD

Since the founding of Israel, successive U.S. administrations have tried various stratagems and tactics to bring about peace between Arabs and Israelis. Despite an outsized investment in diplomatic energy, foreign aid, and presidential prestige, however, this bitter conflict has endured, eroding the U.S. position in the region and undermining American interests.

To understand why the United States has had such a mixed record on Arab-Israeli peacemaking, and to explore what it would take for the United States to help broker peace, the U.S. Institute of Peace convened a study group in 2006–07 with some of America's most experienced senior authorities in the field. Led by Ambassador Daniel C. Kurtzer and anchored by Scott B. Lasensky, William B. Quandt, Steven L. Spiegel, and Shibley I. Telhami, the study group conducted countless hours of confidential interviews in the United States, Europe, and the Middle East with former negotiators, political figures, and civil society leaders from all sides of the conflict. The product of these efforts, *Negotiating Arab-Israeli Peace: American Leadership in the Middle East*, sets forth a compelling, interests-based framework for American engagement in the peace process; provides a critical assessment of U.S. diplomacy since the end of the Cold War; and offers a set of ten core lessons to guide the efforts of future American negotiators.

In this volume, Kurtzer and Lasensky deconstruct America's involvement in the peace process and identify both strengths and weaknesses with respect to policy formulation and execution. Many diplomatic insiders have made valuable contributions to this assessment. *Negotiating Arab-Israeli Peace* is not mired in the details of day-to-day diplomacy nor shaped by the limited perspective of a memoir. Instead, the book is organized thematically to give readers the full scope of the group's experience and expertise. While many of the lessons are derived from the Arab-Israeli context, the book also serves as a general guide for negotiators, academics, and students of conflicts worldwide.

As part of the United States Institute of Peace's congressional mandate to promote research, education, and training on the peaceful management and resolution of international conflicts, *Negotiating Arab-Israeli Peace* is the latest in a distinguished list of volumes the Institute has published on this conflict. In 1991, Sam Lewis and Ken Stein authored *Making Peace Among Arabs and Israelis*, a report that delved deeply into the U.S. negotiating experience during the Cold War. More recently, the Institute has explored the conflict in *How Israelis and Palestinians Negotiate: A Cross-Cultural Analysis of the Oslo Peace Process* edited by Tamara Cofman Wittes, and *Jordanians, Palestinians, and the Hashemite Kingdom in the Middle East Peace Process* by Adnan Abu-Odeh. A recent Special Report on the conflict, *From Rejection to Acceptance: Israeli National Security Thinking and Palestinian Statehood,* was authored by Shlomo Brom.

Negotiating Arab-Israeli Peace represents an important addition to the growing body of scholarship on this seemingly intractable conflict. It provides present and future negotiators with both a resource for assessing past diplomatic efforts and a set of guidelines for shaping future initiatives.

RICHARD H. SOLOMON, PRESIDENT
UNITED STATES INSTITUTE OF PEACE

THE STUDY GROUP ON ARAB-ISRAELI PEACEMAKING

Organization and Members

From its inception in fall 2006, the study group has been chaired and codirected by Daniel Kurtzer, a former U.S. ambassador to Israel and Egypt and currently a professor at Princeton University's Woodrow Wilson School of Public and International Affairs. The project is also codirected by Scott Lasensky, a senior research associate at the U.S. Institute of Peace and acting vice president of the Institute's Center for Conflict Analysis and Prevention.

The study group's work began by forming a core team of some of the most respected academic experts in the United States on Arab-Israeli relations. Professors William Quandt (University of Virginia), Steven Spiegel (University of California, Los Angeles), and Shibley Telhami (University of Maryland and the Brookings Institution) are three of the most widely cited and trusted authorities on the subject. Each has made significant academic contributions and been involved in the policy realm as well. All three have previously contributed to the Institute's program on Arab-Israeli peacemaking. Telhami also served as a member of the Institute's board of directors, and Kurtzer and Quandt were members of the earlier Lewis-Stein project.

Members of the core team were key to the development of this book, which was authored by Kurtzer and Lasensky. Our findings also benefited from the contributions of the project's two special advisers, Ambassador Samuel Lewis and Professor Kenneth Stein.

Since fall 2006 the study group has met with more than one hundred current and former policymakers, parliamentarians, diplomats, academic experts, community leaders, and civil-society figures. Consultations involved not-for-attribution interviews. Meetings were conducted with Americans, Israelis, Arabs, and Europeans. Numerous interviews were conducted in the region. A wide range of opinion shapers and next-generation leaders were also consulted during this process.

On the U.S. side, the study group consulted with virtually every U.S. diplomat and policymaker involved in Arab-Israeli negotiations since the end of the Cold War. There was extremely high interest in meeting with the study group. In addition, consultations were conducted with members of Congress (House and Senate), outside experts, civil-society figures, and community leaders (see full list on page xvii).

Although this book is principally designed as a guidebook for future U.S. negotiators, the findings are also intended to influence the broader policy community and inform public discourse. Arabs and Israelis disagree profoundly on the issues that divide them and what they expect from the United States, but all agree on—and actively seek—a strong U.S. role. Therefore, the publication should also be of interest to the parties themselves, which is why the Institute is committed to promoting the study group's findings in the region.

Profiles of Study Group Members

Daniel Kurtzer, Chair and Codirector

Ambassador Daniel Kurtzer holds the S. Daniel Abraham Chair in Middle East Policy Studies at Princeton University's Woodrow

Wilson School of Public and International Affairs. President Bill Clinton appointed Kurtzer as United States Ambassador to
Egypt, where he served from 1997 to 2001.
President George W. Bush appointed Kurtzer as United States Ambassador to Israel,
where he served from 2001 to 2005. Kurtzer, a thirty-year veteran of the United States
Foreign Service, was an early member of the State Department's
peace team and was deeply involved in the negotiations that led
to the Madrid peace conference. The author of numerous essays
about U.S. diplomacy and the Middle East and a leading public commentator and lecturer, Kurtzer holds a Ph.D. in political
science from Columbia University. In 2006 he worked with the
Institute as an adviser to the Iraq Study Group on regional and
strategic affairs.

Scott Lasensky, Codirector

Dr. Scott Lasensky is a senior research associate at the United States Institute of Peace,
focusing on Arab-Israeli relations and the
regional dimensions of the Iraq crisis. He
is also acting vice president of the Institute's
Center for Conflict Analysis and Prevention.
He has taught courses on Israel, the Middle
East, and U.S. foreign policy at Georgetown
University and Mount Holyoke College. Lasensky was a fellow in
the Studies Program at the Council on Foreign Relations in New
York and a research fellow in foreign policy studies at the Brookings Institution. He holds a Ph.D. in politics from Brandeis University. Lasensky was awarded a Fulbright research fellowship and
was a term member of the Council on Foreign Relations.

William Quandt, Study Group Member

William Quandt holds the Edward R. Stettinius Chair in Politics at the University of Virginia. One of the most widely cited and best-known experts on U.S. policy in the Middle East, North Africa, and the Arab-Israeli conflict, Quandt served on the National Security Council under presidents Richard Nixon and Jimmy Carter and participated in the first Camp David peace summit in 1978. The author of numerous books and articles, his study of U.S. involvement in Arab-Israeli relations, *Peace Process* (Brookings Institution/University of California, third edition, 2005), is a standard text in the field. He has contributed to a number of Institute programs on the Middle East. The recipient of numerous awards and fellowships, Professor Quandt also serves on the Board of Trustees of the American University in Cairo. Quandt received a Ph.D. in political science from the Massachusetts Institute of Technology. In 2006 he worked with the Institute as an adviser to the Iraq Study Group on regional and strategic affairs.

Steven Spiegel, Study Group Member

Steven L. Spiegel, Professor of Political Science at the University of California, Los Angeles (UCLA), is among the world's foremost experts on U.S. foreign policy in the Middle East. He is the director of the Center for Middle East Development (CMED) at UCLA and of Track II Middle East programs at the University of California's Institute on Global Conflict and Cooperation. Widely respected in the United States and throughout the Middle East for his leadership in the field of Track II diplomacy, Spiegel is the author of the award-winning *The Other Arab-Israeli Conflict* (University of Chicago, 1985). He has authored or coauthored over one hundred books, journal articles, and essays, including a major review of contemporary international relations, *World Politics in a New Era*, the fourth edition of which is currently under preparation for Oxford University Press. Dr. Spiegel has advised several presidential campaigns and members of Congress on Arab-Israeli diplomacy. In 2004 and 2005 he was one of three major contributors to the Institute's *Pathways to Peace* initiative on Arab-Israeli diplomacy. Spiegel received a Ph.D. in government from Harvard University.

Shibley Telhami, Study Group Member

Shibley Telhami holds the Anwar Sadat Chair for Peace and Development at the University of Maryland and is a senior fellow in foreign policy studies at the Saban Center at the Brookings Institution. One of the most recognized U.S. experts on the Middle East, Telhami has been consulted by numerous policymakers in several administrations and has testified frequently to Congress. A former adviser to the U.S. Mission to the United Nations, Telhami is the author of numerous books and essays on international affairs and the Middle East. His book, *The Stakes: America and the Middle East*, was selected by *Foreign Affairs* as one of the five best books on the Middle East for 2003. A former Institute board member, Telhami has participated in a wide range of Institute programs on the Middle East. Professor Telhami received a Ph.D. in political science from the University of California, Berkeley. In 2006 he worked with the Institute as an adviser to the Iraq Study Group on regional and strategic affairs.

Interviews and Consultations

United States

Edward Abington
Elliott Abrams
Gary Ackerman
Madeleine Albright
Richard Armitage
James Baker
Samuel Berger
William Burns
Lincoln Chafee
Stephen Cohen
Edward Djerejian
Richard Haass
Gamal Helal
Jeffrey Helsing
Martin Indyk
Herbert Kelman
Daniel Kurtzer
Anthony Lake
Nita Lowey
David Makovsky

Robert Malley
John Marks
Aaron Miller
Robert Pelletreau
Thomas Pickering
Colin Powell
Seymour Reich
Bruce Riedel
Steven Riskin
Dennis Ross
Brent Scowcroft
Steven Spiegel
George Tenet
Toni Verstandig
Edward Walker
Robert Wexler
James Wolfensohn
Anthony Zinni
James Zogby

Arab League

Ismat Abdul Majid   Amr Moussa

Egypt

Ahmad Aboul-Gheit   Dina Khayat
Wa'el Al Assad   Ahmed Maher
Mohammed Bassiouny   Tarek Ragheb
Rawi Camel-Toueg   Nihal Saad
Ali Dessouki   Omar Suleiman
Osama El-Baz

European Union

Marc Otte

Israel

Ami Ayalon   Itzhak Molcho
Moti Cristal   Yohanan Plesner
Shai Feldman   Itamar Rabinovich
Eival Gilady   Jonathan Rynhold
Gidi Grinstein   Ivri Verbin
Dan Meridor   Dov Weisglass
                           Einat Wilf

Jordan

Adnan Abu Odeh   Mohammed al-Masri
Mohammed Abu Ruman   Marwan Muasher
Jawad Anani   Jamil Nimri
Mustafa Hamarneh   Osamha Obeidat
Abdul-Ilah al-Khatib   Ibrahim Seif

Palestinian Authority/PLO

Yasir Abed Rabbo

Ziad Abu Amr

Nisreen Haj Ahmed

Ma'en Areikat

Khaled Elgindy

Saeb Erekat

Salam Fayyad

Akram Hanieh

Samir Huleileh

Issa Kassassieh

Ghassan Khatib

Mouin Rabbani

Mohammed Rachid

Khalil Shikaki

Saudi Arabia

Adel al-Jubeir

Syria

Riad Daoudi

Ziad Haidar

Ibrahim Hamidi

Marwan Kabalan

Hind Aboud Kabawat

Walid Mouallem

Sami Moubayed

Bouthaina Shaaban

Farouk al-Shara

Samir al-Taqi

United Nations

Terje Rød-Larsen

ACKNOWLEDGMENTS

The authors are deeply grateful to a number of people whose assistance was invaluable to this project. First and foremost, we owe a debt of gratitude to the other three members of our core study group—William Quandt, Steven Spiegel, and Shibley Telhami—also known as our dream team. They demonstrated a commitment, seriousness, and intelligence that place them in a league of their own.

Many individuals at the United States Institute of Peace were essential to our work. Ambassador Richard Solomon, the Institute's president, was generous with his support and intellectual guidance. Executive vice president Patricia Thomson and vice presidents Paul Stares and David Smock were committed to this project from its inception, and former vice president Paul Stares was an early advocate of this effort. Without the assistance and support of Michael Graham and his budget team and Valerie Norville and the publications department, the project would not have functioned so smoothly. Members of the Institute's Arab-Israeli conflict team offered valuable input and generous support at every stage.

Jamie Arnett and Robert Grace provided critical research and program support. Their devotion to this initiative often went beyond the nine-to-five routine. We extend our special appreciation to Rob for shepherding the publication of this volume.

Ambassador Samuel Lewis and Professor Kenneth Stein served as special advisers, a fitting and well-deserved title. Our work would not have been possible without the cooperation we received from approximately one hundred current and former policymakers, parliamentarians, diplomats, and civil-society leaders—Americans, Arabs, Israelis, and Europeans—who were consulted for the project, and to whom we owe our appreciation for their time and candor.

An external, academic reviewer provided extensive comments, which we appreciate. We also wish to thank the many colleagues at the Institute and elsewhere—too many to name here—who commented on various drafts, offered advice, and shared research materials.

At the Woodrow Wilson School of Public and International Affairs at Princeton University, thanks to Dean Anne-Marie Slaughter for her support of the Abraham chair and this project.

On a personal note, a special word of gratitude to our wives, Sheila Doppelt Kurtzer and Elise Pressma Lasensky, whose support was a key ingredient of this project. For their love and advice, we are deeply indebted.

As the authors of this study, we take sole responsibility for its content.

AMBASSADOR DANIEL KURTZER, PH.D.
Lecturer and S. Daniel Abraham Professor in Middle Eastern Policy Studies, Woodrow Wilson School of Public and International Affairs, Princeton University, Princeton, NJ

SCOTT LASENSKY, PH.D.
Acting Vice President, Center for Conflict Analysis and Prevention, United States Institute of Peace, Washington, DC

January 2008

LESSONS IGNORED, OPPORTUNITIES LOST

One hundred, two hundred years from now, historians will look back at American foreign policy towards the [Arab-Israeli] conflict … and wonder why we let this thing drag on, bleeding and damaging us, when we had so much potential influence over the parties.

—Former senior National Security Council official

When the United States Institute of Peace published Ambassador Samuel Lewis and Professor Kenneth Stein's *Making Peace among Arabs and Israelis* in 1991, there was great hope for progress toward a comprehensive Arab-Israeli settlement. With the end of the Cold War, the U.S.-led victory in the first Gulf War, and the general decline in opposition to peace throughout the region, the strategic environment seemed propitious for the United States to lead the Middle East peace process into a new phase. Earlier U.S. successes in mediating Israeli-Egyptian peace and Israeli-Syrian disengagement were a promising record on which to build. From the early 1970s, U.S. leadership, agile diplomacy led by the president and secretary of state, and the sustained and judicious deployment of the full range of U.S. diplomatic resources led reluctant parties to negotiated agreements. By the early 1990s, a comprehensive Arab-Israeli peace—actively promoted by the United States—seemed more real than at any time in a half-century. But nearly twenty years later, the record is largely one of failure.

At the height of the Cold War, the need for a U.S-led Arab-Israeli peace process was unmistakable. Washington responded, and our achievements helped to tilt the strategic balance to the United States' favor. In 1970, Secretary of State William Rogers developed a cease-fire plan that brought the Egyptian-Israeli "war of attrition" to an end. Out of the devastation and destruction of the October 1973 Arab-Israeli war, the Richard Nixon and Gerald Ford administrations fashioned a U.S.-led peace process based on a step-by-step strategy rather than on grand designs and comprehensive formulas. When these negotiations over interim arrangements broke down, Washington often stepped in and provided political assurances, economic assistance, or security guarantees, in effect offering the parties what they could not obtain directly from each other. This negotiating formula yielded two Egyptian-Israeli disengagement agreements and a Syrian-Israeli disengagement accord. Egyptian president Anwar Sadat's surprise visit to Jerusalem in 1977 and his address to the Israeli parliament demonstrated that leadership remained a critical precondition to peacemaking. But even bold leadership could not bridge all the divides. Israeli-Egyptian peace would require intensive U.S. mediation, including the direct intervention of President Jimmy Carter at the Camp David summit in 1978 and in the months that followed. With Egypt firmly in the American camp, and a new "special" relationship with Israel, the Egyptian-Israeli peace treaty helped to shift the political tide in the region away from Moscow and toward Washington.

Still, for years, the Arab and Muslim worlds would remain split between rejectionist forces and those willing to recognize Israel and support an Arab-Israeli peace process. The very notion of incrementalism and step-by-step negotiations came under attack. The second part of the Camp David accords—the provisions for Palestinian autonomy—went unfulfilled. As the Cold War intensified in the 1980s and instability increased in Lebanon and the Persian Gulf, the setting for Arab-Israeli peacemaking again turned hostile. President Ronald Reagan in 1982 and Secretary of State George Shultz in 1988 tried to jump-start peace talks through U.S.-drafted plans, but both efforts failed to win Israeli or Arab support. Following nearly seven years of peace process inactivity, Palestinians launched the first Intifada in 1987, reflecting their frustration over continued occupation and the absence of movement toward peace.

With the end of the Cold War and the U.S.-led victory against Saddam Hussein in 1991, the strategic balance once again shifted in the United States' favor and conditions were amenable to reviving the peace process. Determined U.S. diplomatic leadership brought Arabs and Israelis together in the 1991 Madrid peace conference, which cemented the U.S. role as the sole power broker in the region, launched a region-wide peace and reconciliation effort, and resulted in direct bilateral and multilateral negotiations between Israel and its Arab neighbors. In 1994, Israel and Jordan signed an enduring peace agreement, but the rest of the process remained deeply troubled and ultimately witnessed the spectacular collapse of both the Israeli-Syrian and the Israeli-Palestinian peace processes at the end of the decade, the latter leaving thousands dead in its wake.

Today, the aftermath of the terrorist attacks of September 11, 2001, the deepening crisis in Iraq, and the looming confrontation with Iran suggest a similar strategic need for an active U.S. approach toward what is undoubtedly one of the world's most pernicious regional conflicts. On the surface, the George W. Bush (Bush 43) administration seems to have belatedly acknowledged the need for U.S. leadership in the Arab-Israeli peace process. But this came after six and a half years of neglect and a high toll in human suffering.

An analysis of the entire period since the end of the Cold War—the focus of this study—reveals an alarming pattern of mismanaged diplomacy. Missteps in U.S. diplomacy have been both strategic and tactical, and it is essential for the next generation of U.S. negotiators to learn from them and improve the United States' ability to negotiate Arab-Israeli peace. Flaws in U.S. diplomacy stretching back to the Clinton administration have contributed to the worst crisis in Arab-Israeli relations in a generation. This devastating failure has hurt U.S. interests and damaged our ability to gain cooperation from allies and key regional players. At the popular level, it has weakened the U.S. position in the region and on the world stage. It has also jeopardized our long-term investment in Arab-Israeli peace.

Failed diplomacy, combined with regional players' own missteps, has cost the region even more. With the collapse of the Oslo process in 2000, thousands of Israelis and Palestinians lost their lives and tens of thousands were injured in waves of violence that deeply scarred both societies. The so-called peace camp in Israel collapsed. Increasing lawlessness, abject poverty, and civil strife came to define the Palestinian territories. Instability in Lebanon, where Israel and Hezbollah fought a month-long war in mid-2006, continues to threaten the regional order. Syria and Israel have failed to resume negotiations, broken off since 2000. The diplomatic landscape has been altered so dramatically that the Bush 43 administration for a time actively discouraged Israel from responding to Syrian peace overtures.

The very fabric of the peace process—the formal peace treaties between Israel and Egypt and Israel and Jordan—is increasingly under pressure. On each track, the peace has turned colder, with few meaningful civil-society or business links. In Jordan, the crisis in the Palestinian territories together with the U.S. occupation of Iraq and the resulting influx of Iraqi refugees have weakened King Abdullah and destabilized the kingdom.

The failure of peacemaking is most noticeable, however, on the Israeli-Palestinian track. The accession of Hamas to power in the Palestinian legislative elections in January 2006 and its violent takeover of Gaza in mid-2007 highlight how dramatic the deterioration has been since Madrid and Oslo. Many people are talking about the end of the possibility of a two-state solution to the Israeli-Palestinian conflict. In the 1990s, it was suggested that the Arab-Israeli peace process was progressive—that is, that advances were irreversible. But events since 2000 have challenged that notion. The process is far more fragile than was previously believed. The clock can indeed be turned back.

How did we arrive at such a sorry state of affairs? Since the Madrid peace conference in 1991—a watershed in Arab-Israeli peacemaking—failures of U.S. diplomacy have outweighed successes. Stronger and more effective diplomacy could have increased the prospects for successful peacemaking during the 1990s and stemmed the steep deterioration in Arab-Israeli ties following the collapse of the Oslo process in 2000–2001. Instead, Washington disengaged, allowing the conflict to fester and deepen. U.S. involvement has been characterized by fits and starts, errors of omission and commission, and fundamental weaknesses in policy formulation and execution. Rhetoric all too often has replaced action. Washington has tried quite hard to keep the process, feeble as it may be, under its control, but the lack of effective, adept diplomacy—coupled with deteriorating conditions on the ground—has invited increased activity, largely directed against peace, from a wide range of regional actors and third parties, including Iran. The lessons of earlier diplomatic achievements have been ignored or unlearned. When diplomacy stumbled and new lessons could have been absorbed, more often than not the United States failed to adapt. Opportunities were squandered, potential breakthroughs missed, and meaningful advances stalled unnecessarily.

Fortunately, this is not where the story ends. Despite the set-backs of recent years, Washington still has an enormous reservoir of influence with the parties. Our earlier successes in Arab-Israeli peacemaking are a reminder—to both the parties and ourselves—of what effective diplomacy can accomplish. Public opinion in the region continues largely to support a renewed peace process. The steep decline in relations between Israel and the Palestinians may be reversing, as politics realign on both sides and interest in negotiations resurfaces after a seven-year hiatus. Should the United States resume an active diplomatic role, it will enjoy the support of a wide array of actors, from the European Union and the United Nations to key regional players such as Saudi Arabia and Egypt. Rejectionist forces, be they Palestinian groups such as Hamas and Palestinian Islamic Jihad, or Hezbollah in Leba-non, or Iran, remain formidable. But rarely has there been such a groundswell of untapped regional and international support for the United States to mount a major diplomatic initiative.

The task will not be easy, however. Success will depend on heeding the lessons of the past—laid out in the body of this study—and will also require U.S. negotiators to have a clear sense of the changing context that surrounds Arab-Israeli peacemaking, on the ground, across the region, and within the broader strategic environment. Last and perhaps most important, our negotiators must approach their task with a keen understanding of the indis-pensability of the United States to the process and the unique role we can play in resolving the Arab-Israeli conflict.

Changing Context

From a historical perspective, U.S. negotiators face a set of Arab-Israeli relationships that has become more complicated over time, particularly on the Israeli-Palestinian track, as the sheer complexity of the issues that remain to be resolved—such as Jerusalem and borders, as well as the potential spoiler role of Hamas—pose a greater challenge than in earlier periods. The exponential growth of Israeli settlements over the last two decades, to take just one example, suggests that negotiated solutions will be harder to achieve, not to mention more costly. These complications also extend to the role of the United States and other third parties on the ground, whether in peacekeeping or humanitarian assistance, in which outside interventions are likely to be far more intensive than they were in earlier phases of the peace process. Whether in the Palestinian territories, on the Israel-Lebanon border, or on the Golan Heights, more robust third-party involvement will define future negotiations, agreements, and interventions.

As the Arab-Israeli relationship has become more complex, political power has also become more fragmented, both within societies and across the region, making peace negotiations more difficult. It was easier for Sadat, the established leader of a regional power, to recognize Israel's legitimacy and receive all of Sinai in return than it was more than a decade later for the Palestine Liberation Organization (PLO) leadership to negotiate with Israel, to say nothing of today's post–Yasir Arafat Palestinian leadership, which has ruptured along generational and ideological fault lines. Similarly, it was easier for Israel to return Sinai—an area of strategic and economic importance, but with little religious or historical significance—in exchange for a peace treaty with Egypt than it was (and remains) for Israel to compromise with Palestinian leaders on territory, Jerusalem, and other issues with deep religious and ideological overtones that cut to core definitions of national identity. On the Syrian track, the contrast in leadership is also notable, as the regime of Bashar Assad is firmly in control, but weaker, less predictable, and more narrowly based than was his father's rule.

The difficulty in peace negotiations brought about by political fragmentation extends to U.S. diplomacy. The Carter administration dealt with Sadat and Menachem Begin, strong leaders capable of compromise. The Clinton administration worked with Yitzhak Rabin and King Hussein of Jordan, similarly determined leaders who could conclude a permanent Israeli-Jordanian peace. But since the late 1990s, the leadership stratum has weakened. The Israeli and Palestinian political systems have been torn apart by domestic divides and violent conflict, leaving leaders on both sides less able to make the kinds of compromises that earlier Middle Eastern leaders made. The fragmenting of political power is seen most dramatically in Iraq, Lebanon, and the Palestinian territories. As the importance of nonstate actors continues to grow, the challenge for an outside party such as the United States is not merely to contain and defeat extremist and rejectionist groups, but also to engage and moderate those actors—including Islamists— whose support will be needed to achieve durable solutions.

With fragmentation has also come greater interconnectedness among the region's conflicts, including Iraq, the Arab-Israeli sphere, Lebanon, and Iran. These conflicts are increasingly linked not just to each other but also to shifting power trends in the region, such as the economic rise of the Arab Gulf and the surge in Iranian and Shia power. Although the changing context may appear daunting to future negotiators, it also underscores why Arab-Israeli peacemaking is so vital.

For the United States, Arab-Israeli peacemaking is crucial to our own national security interests. Counterterrorism priorities since the September 11 attacks would be easier to pursue if the Arab-Israeli conflict could be alleviated. Washington's interest in economic and political reform in the greater Middle East is complicated by Arab-Israeli strife. The U.S. interest in mitigating Islamist militancy would also be better served by a renewed peace process, as would the need for greater regional cooperation on Iraq and nuclear nonproliferation. Moreover, the conflict has destabilized other parts of the region that remain critical to the United States, such as Lebanon. Most obvious, the U.S. commitment to Israel's security and well-being is best served by moving toward, rather than away from, a comprehensive Arab-Israeli peace settlement.

Why the United States Remains Indispensable

In addition to our own strategic interests in achieving a comprehensive Arab-Israeli peace settlement—including our commitment to Israel—there is another reason why the U.S. role is indispensable, particularly on the Palestinian track, which remains the heart of the conflict. Simply stated, large asymmetries of power require a robust third-party role. Power dynamics in the Israeli-Palestinian conflict are deeply unbalanced, leaving the parties unable to reach viable negotiated arrangements on their own. In this respect, the U.S. role toward the Palestinians adds a dimension to our diplomacy between Israel and its neighboring Arab states.

Israel is an established sovereign state with a robust, thriving economy and a world-class military; Palestinians remain under occupation, bereft of effective public institutions, highly dependent on international economic assistance, lacking basic security, and incapable of providing the full measure of security to which Israelis are entitled. The eventual collapse of the Oslo process—which was initiated and defined by the parties without U.S. intervention—best exemplifies the general rule that, left on their own, the parties cannot address the deep, structural impediments to peace.

That is why the United States is indispensable. As the principal

outside actor, it is the task of the United States to facilitate, mediate, and to some degree arbitrate and oversee the negotiations,
to cut through the asymmetries and help the parties address each
other's needs. For Israel, the core issue has long been security. In
earlier eras, U.S. diplomacy was successful because we found ways
to provide Israel with the security goods it required—that is, security assurances, military aid, economic assistance, and peacekeeping resources—while also addressing the requirements of the
Arab side. These U.S. inducements allowed Israel to take risks
for peace, including risks designed to assure both its security and
the character of the state. As a result, and despite long-standing
negative attitudes toward other outside actors, Israeli leaders and
the Israeli public have developed an intense and profound sense
of confidence and trust in the United States. For Palestinians, the
core issue remains the establishment of an independent, viable
state, and the United States must help address the asymmetry of
power toward this end.

However, throughout much of the period from the early 1990s
to the present, Washington has reinforced rather than ameliorated
some of the most fundamental asymmetries between Israel and
the Palestinians. In 2002, the United States explicitly recognized
the Palestinian need for a viable state and made repeated refer-
ences to such a goal. But since then, the United States has watched
as developments in the region seriously undermined that objective. The United States did not push back when Israel redefined
contiguity of territory to mean transportation linkages between
Palestinian areas instead of territorial linkages.

On the Syria-Israel track, the United States has done nothing
since 2001 to promote a settlement or offer ideas on the complex
set of issues that still divide the parties. Not only do both sides
need Washington to get back to where negotiations left off, but
the United States is central to each side's vision of implementation and a post-conflict peace and security regime. Before 2001,

the United States pushed the parties aggressively toward peace, though at key junctures Washington simply conveyed the position of one party to the other, adding no value in bridging proposals.

In some circles, it has become fashionable to downplay the role of the United States in Arab-Israeli negotiations; according to this view, the conflict and its possible resolution are largely issues between the parties. The Begin-Sadat, Peres-Arafat, or Rabin-Hussein channels are sometimes cited as proof that the U.S. role is not critical. But such a perspective belies political realities, not to mention the lessons of decades of diplomacy.

To be sure, the parties themselves bear primary responsibility for resolving the conflict, but the United States has long held an outsized role. When the parties have created their own momentum in the negotiations, as was the case with Sadat's visit to Jerusalem or the signing of the Oslo agreement, they have always leaned on Washington to help them bridge differences, walk the last mile, provide off-the-table incentives to reach agreement, and to be an involved stakeholder in implementing accords. When the parties have been far apart, as they have been in recent years, U.S. involvement can be the difference between conflict escalation and conflict management. When the United States steps back, as it did during the second Intifada and the 2006 Israel-Hezbollah war, conflict can widen and be prolonged. Unlike other outside actors, Washington is already deeply enmeshed—politically, strategically, and economically—across the entire set of Arab-Israeli relationships.

Origins of the Study

Given Washington's central role, not to mention the growing chorus calling for greater U.S. diplomatic engagement, the Institute

placed a great deal of importance on appraising the U.S. negotiating experience. More than fifteen years had passed since the
publication of an earlier Institute study, further strengthening the
case for a new effort. In fall 2006, the Institute established the
Study Group on Arab-Israeli Peacemaking, chaired by Ambassador Daniel Kurtzer, former U.S. ambassador to Egypt and Israel,
currently a professor at Princeton University's Woodrow Wilson
School of Public and International Affairs. This book, which fo-
cuses solely on the U.S. role since the end of the Cold War, offers
the project's first set of findings. As the study suggests, there is a
great deal more that can and should be done to promote U.S.
interests and improve the prospects for Arab-Israeli peace. The
parties themselves, not to mention other outside actors, share the
blame for the failures in peacemaking, and by itself, U.S. involvement does not dictate the course of events. That said, Washington
is far from being a bystander. Our influence in determining the
course of Arab-Israeli relations remains substantial.

From the project's inception, Ambassador Kurtzer has served
as both project chair and codirector, together with Scott Lasensky,
a senior research associate and acting vice president of the Institute's Center for Conflict Analysis and Prevention. They are the
authors of this book.

Members of the core study group include three of the leading
and most well-respected academic experts on the conflict, professors William B. Quandt (University of Virginia), Shibley Telhami
(University of Maryland), and Steven L. Spiegel (University of
California, Los Angeles). Through a year-long process of consultation and fact finding, the study group met with over one hundred decision makers, diplomats, and civil-society figures, including several former secretaries of state, national security advisers,
and members of Congress. We examined an array of primary and
secondary sources, consulted informally with a range of outside

experts, and traveled to the region to meet with a wide range of personalities in Egypt, Syria, Jordan, Israel, and the Palestinian territories. All five members of the team were deeply involved at every stage of the project. A list of consultations and interviews, as well as a more detailed description of the study group and its activities, is included in this publication.[1]

The book is organized as follows. Following this introduction is a short chapter that examines each of the three most recent U.S. administrations: George H.W. Bush (Bush 41), Clinton, and Bush 43. The third section—the core of the book—puts forward a series of lessons, organized thematically and intended to guide the next generation of U.S. negotiators. The book concludes with a set of recommendations for future administrations.

In addition to the lessons laid out in this publication, the study group may continue its work and offer in-depth examinations of several pivotal periods in Arab-Israeli negotiations. The focus would be on historical moments about which the first crop of memoirs has left more questions than answers, and about which the initial wave of analytical work remains incomplete. Given that the study group's extensive consultations shed new light on a number of pivotal moments in the negotiations, members felt that a need still exists for additional contributions. Debates in recent years have produced great disagreement about what transpired at key decision points after Madrid. For a conflict so laden with history, in which the diplomatic record weighs heavily on future negotiations, a detached, detailed, and dispassionate account of recent diplomacy is sorely needed.

---

1. During its deliberations, the study group reached out to an even wider variety of personalities. When we were unable to confer directly with key players, published interviews, memoirs, and the personal accounts of study group members were consulted.

THE UNITED STATES AND ARAB-ISRAELI PEACEMAKING
A Report Card

From the early 1990s to the present, the track record of U.S. diplomacy in the Arab-Israeli conflict has become progressively worse. Overall, though the record of the Bush 41 administration is not flawless, it gets the highest marks for both performance and outcomes. The Bush 41 team benefited from a highly effective foreign policy process and a uniquely advantageous strategic environment. Clinton invested heavily in Arab-Israeli peacemaking, particularly at the end of his administration, and can claim some achievements. He was far more successful than his predecessor at building a strong coalition within the United States to support U.S. peacemaking efforts. But his policies contributed to significant diplomatic failures, and the policy process was often dysfunctional and less effective than was Bush 41's. The Bush 43 administration had the fewest successes. Admittedly, the negotiating environment was the most challenging under Bush 43, but the dismal track record on Arab-Israeli peacemaking stemmed from other, more discretionary factors.

Bush 41 had the clearest sense of strategy, which the administration pursued in a highly disciplined, committed, and effective manner. Diplomacy was active and sustained, emanating from policy that the president prioritized and clearly articulated. When the negotiating environment was unfavorable, as in the administration's first year, the Bush 41 team sought to create opportunities and presented new ideas to the parties. When a window of opportunity opened following the first Gulf War, Bush 41 ex-

ploited the favorable strategic environment as part of a concerted regional diplomatic initiative. During both periods, full consultations with all key players informed and shaped U.S. policy.
These consultations gave the Bush 41 team a clear sense of both
the needs and constraints of the parties; Secretary of State James
Baker was careful not to allow politics in the region to wield a veto
over U.S. policy decisions.

Throughout the Bush 41 years, Baker remained firmly in control of peace process diplomacy, drawing on a diverse and experienced team of policy planners, negotiators, and diplomats in the
field. Bush 41's achievements in launching the Madrid process
were both substantive and procedural. Bush 41 and Baker also
had a keen sense of when U.S. diplomacy needed to be scaled
back. Following the Madrid conference in 1991, bilateral and
multilateral negotiations were launched. From the outset, it was
clear that the bilateral negotiations were in trouble. It took weeks
for Israelis and Palestinians even to enter the conference room
in Washington, as the two sides wrangled over procedural issues.
Neither Israelis nor Arabs seemed fundamentally interested in negotiating. In an election year in both Israel and the United States,
the Bush 41 administration understood that its scope to play an
active third-party role was limited, and temporarily backed away,
as evidenced by Secretary Baker's lack of involvement in the process following Madrid.

Another factor, which amounted to a Bush 41 weakness, was
the administration's failure to build a strong coalition at home to
support its strategy. This deficiency hobbled our diplomatic efforts and stoked domestic distrust. Some domestic advocates for
Israel were unnecessarily alienated, most notably around the loan
guarantees dispute, in which the United States made Israel's request for preferential financing contingent on a settlements freeze.
The political fallout from the sharp disagreements with the Yit-

zhak Shamir government, particularly over settlements—and the White House's decision to dig in its heels against their continued expansion—had a searing effect that far outlasted the Bush 41 administration, reverberating well into the Clinton and Bush 43 years and causing the next president and his team to overcompensate in ways that created a different set of problems. The Bush 41 administration deserves credit for taking a firm stance on settlement expansion, an issue that had long undermined Arab trust in the peace process and increased Israel's own vulnerabilities. However, by carrying over this policy disagreement into an all-out confrontation with the organized U.S. Jewish community, the administration weakened its ability to play an active role later on.

The Clinton administration inherited an ideal strategic environment for peacemaking. The United States was the sole superpower and had successfully conducted the 1991 Gulf War, building an Arab coalition to support it. The Madrid conference was an impetus to peacemaking, including the multilateral process that brought Arab states into the negotiations. Finally, Israel had a new prime minister in Yitzhak Rabin, replacing Shamir, who admitted later that he never intended to negotiate peace seriously with Palestinians.

Clinton supported peace efforts during his first term, although his direct involvement did not become a major factor until his second term. During the Clinton presidency, the United States enjoyed enhanced prestige in the region and on the international stage, and Arab-Israeli peacemaking was the centerpiece of the Clinton team's regional strategy. Members of the administration understood the priority assigned to the peace process and shared a common commitment. In contrast to Bush 41, Clinton built a strong and diverse domestic coalition to support U.S. leadership in the peace process.

However, the Clinton approach was less disciplined and less

strategic than was Bush 41's, and our study group heard from both Israeli and Arab officials that the administration's approach appeared to lack focus and follow-through. The Clinton administration left in place a bilateral negotiating structure, which had run its course the previous year, and invested precious little in multilateral negotiations, an arena that had brought substantial Arab state support and involvement to the peace process for the first time. Moreover, the administration knew about but largely ignored—and thus failed to shape—the secret contacts between Israel and the PLO that were to result in the Oslo accords.[2]

Ignoring the Oslo channel was due in part to an early decision by the Clinton team to prioritize the Israel-Syria track of negotiations. Sidelining the Palestinian track was itself a questionable decision. But even with its focus on Syria, the administration failed to exploit a potential opening when Rabin secretly told Secretary of State Warren Christopher and envoy Dennis Ross in the summer of 1993 that Israel was willing to negotiate a full withdrawal from the Golan Heights in exchange for full peace and agreed security arrangements with Syria. With Rabin's hypothetical offer in hand, the United States did not mount a sustained diplomatic shuttle effort, as had been done in the past. The so-called Rabin deposit was ultimately squandered.

Even after Oslo was signed in a White House–sponsored ceremony, the United States was largely hands-off on the Palestinian track for almost two years, leaving the hard bargaining to the parties. Washington declined to settle disputes or monitor performance. The administration's eleventh-hour intervention in mid-1995 did help to finalize the Interim Agreement, also known as

2. In the landmark 1993 agreement, Israel and the PLO formally recognized each other and agreed to establish a five-year interim period of Palestinian self-rule. Oslo also marked the first time both sides agreed to negotiate over all the core issues, including Jerusalem, refugees, and settlements, albeit only after the establishment of Palestinian autonomy. See Appendix for the text of the Oslo accords.

Oslo II, which set forth the nuts and bolts of Palestinian self-rule and committed Israel to a series of withdrawals from Palestinian territory. But for the most part, Clinton and senior administration officials were not deeply engaged until very late in the process.

The October 1998 Wye summit, for which Clinton brought Benjamin Netanyahu and Arafat together to rescue the process from collapse, represented a different, more activist approach, with the United States taking on the role of arbitrator and moving the parties to adopt U.S. bridging proposals. But Wye proved to be the exception, not the rule. Early inaction by the president and his team, together with the administration's failure to hold Israelis and Palestinians accountable to the agreements they signed, were to have far-reaching negative consequences for the peace process and for U.S. policy. The Clinton team focused intensely, even obsessively, on keeping the Israeli-Palestinian track alive and maintaining momentum in the talks, but at the expense of debilitating actions by the parties—Palestinian violence and incitement, Israeli settlement expansion, Palestinian Authority (PA) corruption, and constant backsliding by both sides—that ultimately overwhelmed and defeated the process.

Ehud Barak's election in 1999 gave the Clinton team another opportunity to seek a comprehensive settlement, a rare second chance in diplomacy, but Washington failed to capitalize on this opportunity. Clinton's most ambitious diplomatic initiatives—including the early-2000 push for an Israeli-Syrian peace treaty and the late-2000 U.S. parameters for an Israeli-Palestinian deal—came too late, appeared rushed and ill-prepared, and were too easily thrown off balance by resistance from either Israelis or Arabs. The proper groundwork was not laid for the last-ditch summit meetings with Israelis and Syrians at Shepherdstown, West Virginia, and with the Syrians at Geneva. The United States came to the table without its own clear ideas for resolving the remaining points of disagreement.

The most glaring failure of this period was the ill-conceived Camp David II summit in July 2000, for which Clinton brought Barak and Arafat to the presidential retreat to sign a framework agreement on a final peace treaty. After nearly two weeks, the summit collapsed with no agreement. A contributing factor to the failure of Camp David, and U.S. diplomacy more generally, was a policy process that was too insular and inhibited the development of U.S. positions on the core issues. Therefore, it was not surprising that when negotiations eventually reached this stage, the United States was unprepared, and our negotiators scrambled at the last minute to put together U.S. positions on complex issues such as Jerusalem and borders. The parameters, which were Clinton's ideas for bridging the major divides separating Israelis and Palestinians, were withheld until the administration's final days in office. Clinton's stipulation that the initiative would expire at the end of his term, which was intended to pressure the parties, predictably had the opposite effect.[3]

The Clinton years also suffered from sharp confrontations between the administration and the Republican-controlled Congress, which often spilled over into foreign policy, including Arab-Israeli diplomacy. At certain moments, particularly when questions of settlements, foreign aid, or Jerusalem were debated, the lack of bipartisan support was a drain on our peacemaking. But Clinton's leadership on the issue, especially his constant courting of Jewish-American interest groups, gave the administration a strong base of domestic support, proving that a president who lays the proper groundwork at home enjoys much more room to maneuver abroad. Clinton's commitment and personal dedication to Arab-Israeli peace gave him lasting popularity throughout the region, demonstrating the desire for sustained U.S. involvement in the process.

---

3. Shortly after Clinton left office, the parameters were disavowed by the Bush 43 administration. See Appendix for the text of the Clinton parameters.

The Bush 43 approach to the conflict lacked both commitment and a sense of strategic purpose. Some in the administration dismissed the importance of the Arab-Israeli conflict, suggesting that it was subsidiary to removing the Saddam Hussein regime and pressing for far-reaching social and political reforms in the Arab world. The road to Jerusalem, it was argued, went through Baghdad. Most damaging to U.S. interests, Bush 43 policies left the widely held perception that the United States had disengaged from active peacemaking. This impression influenced not only the prospects for peace but also severely eroded the United States' regional standing.

Despite a very negative environment for peacemaking in 2001–2002, opportunities presented themselves in the form of the Mitchell report[4] (April 2001) and the impact of September 11 on regional attitudes, but the Bush 43 administration did not respond. Throughout his two terms, Bush 43 failed to create or exploit other opportunities, such as the Arab League peace initiative that led to the Beirut Declaration, the election of Palestinian president Mahmoud Abbas, or the Israeli withdrawal from Gaza. Overall, the administration appeared content to articulate policy positions and then move to the sidelines and await outcomes.

When Washington did engage actively, disagreements among senior officials undermined U.S. diplomacy, as did repeated counsel from senior administration figures to remain on the sidelines. When major initiatives were put forward, as with the Roadmap peace plan in 2003, they were not aggressively pursued, not monitored, and lacked sustained diplomatic engagement. Backed by the so-called Quartet of the United States supported by the European Union, Russia, and the United Nations, the Roadmap was released with fanfare just after the overthrow of Saddam Hussein and set forth an ambitious three-stage, performance-based plan

4. See this book's Web site at www.usip.org for the text of the Mitchell report.

to stabilize Israeli-Palestinian relations, bolster Palestinian institutions, and move the parties back to negotiations over a two-state settlement. But no sustained attempt was made to implement the initiative. Its ambitious goals and timelines were effectively abandoned.

The Bush 43 administration achieved some of its goals for Palestinian reform, including streamlined and transparent PA public finances and the establishment in 2003 of a prime minister's office, but made no effort to leverage these advances to revive the peace process. Mahmoud Abbas, who was elected president in January 2005 after Arafat's death, repeatedly asked for more tangible U.S. support to strengthen his hand in internal Palestinian decision-making and create more political space for engaging Israel. The administration did not respond in a meaningful way. In fact, the constant emphasis on Palestinian institution building, divorced from the political process, appeared to some as a substitute for active mediation. A variety of envoys were appointed, but they did not have full administration support, had their missions too narrowly defined, or both. The administration pushed hard for Palestinian legislative elections in 2006, only to be surprised at the Hamas victory. For the next year, the White House sought to undermine the Hamas government, and opposed all attempts to form a Palestinian unified government.

There was activity during the Bush 43 years—including the abovementioned Roadmap initiative, the appointment of several envoys, and summit meetings—but being busy is not the same as being actively engaged and moving the overall process forward. By effectively moving to the sidelines during these years, the United States did not increase the pressure on the parties to reach their own solution. Instead, the divide between Arabs and Israelis widened.

None of the administrations under review effectively consulted with former officials, retired diplomats, or outside experts. In earlier periods there was more exchange with those who did not have official positions in government, but who had experience and knowledge that could contribute to administration decision-making. Those who happen to be in government do not necessarily have a lock on wisdom or ideas, and we believe that the gradual end of the pattern of outside consultation contributed to past lessons being lost, along with the potential that opportunities presented.

Making Peace among Arabs and Israelis
Lessons Learned and Relearned

Drawing from a year-long process of consultation, ten lessons were identified to guide Arab-Israeli peacemaking for future U.S. negotiators. These conclusions are offered as the consensus judgment of the study group. The lessons are organized thematically, focusing on the strategic context, the substance of Arab-Israeli diplomacy, and the policy process and domestic context within which U.S. diplomacy is developed and implemented.

There are no magic formulas or quick fixes to apply to the situation. Successful diplomacy often requires adaptation, improvisation, and learning. The lessons are thus both proscriptive and prescriptive, and emerge from what is now known about the overall narrative of U.S. involvement since 1990, when the earlier Institute study was published. The views expressed represent only those of the authors and the study group, and not necessarily the views of anyone with whom we consulted.

The Strategic Context

> [The conflict] is a core issue.... I don't see how anybody can deny that, and it has been for years.... If we are seen to be trying to deal with the Arab-Israeli conflict, we will have much more credibility with many of the actors that are important in what's going on in Iraq.
> —Former secretary of state

Lesson 1. Arab-Israeli peacemaking is in our national interest: September 11, Iraq, and increasing instability in the Middle East have made U.S. leadership in the peace process more, not less, important. The president needs to indicate that the peace process is a priority and ensure that the administration acts accordingly.

For decades, successive U.S. administrations have assigned a high priority to resolving the Arab-Israeli conflict. Both Republican and Democratic presidents have understood the importance of ending the conflict, or at least managing and containing its impact, and have been cognizant of the effect that U.S. engagement in peace diplomacy has had on our other interests in the region. The relative importance of the issue within the broader strategic environment has evolved over time. During the Cold War, the Arab-Israeli question intersected sharply with high-order U.S. national security interests at particular moments, such as the 1956 Suez Crisis and the October 1973 war. Successful U.S. diplomacy often carried with it monumental strategic benefits, as in Washington's shuttle diplomacy in the mid-1970s and the 1979 Israel-Egypt peace treaty, both of which sharply reduced the Soviet role in the region.

In the present strategic environment, defined most notably by the threat from al Qaeda, the broader struggle against Islamist militancy, and the ongoing challenges of the U.S. occupation of Iraq, Arab-Israeli peacemaking has become even more important. The interconnectedness of strategic factors is as complex today, if not more so, than in earlier phases of the peace process, though the connections themselves are new and still emerging. There are some who reject this proposition and place far less emphasis on ending the conflict. According to this school of thought, which had strong supporters in the Bush 43 administration, U.S. priorities lie in transformational diplomacy and democracy promotion. Adherents to this perspective argue that broader social and political change in the Arab world is a necessary precondition to resolving the Arab-Israeli conflict. They dismiss the notion of engaging with actors viewed as adversaries of the United States, preferring policies of isolation and coercion—one reason why they assign limited importance to ending the conflict.

Our findings suggest that this is a deeply flawed approach. The increasingly negative effect of the Arab-Israeli conflict on the broader strategic environment facing the United States was a common and constant theme in consultations and interviews. The conflict remains one of the most pernicious and evocative in the Arab and Muslim worlds, and though it is not directly linked to September 11 or Iraq, as some have inaccurately asserted, resolving it will help the United States respond to other strategic priorities.

As the proliferation of information technologies, especially the Internet and satellite television, has coincided with a spike in Arab-Israeli violence, the profile of the Arab-Israeli conflict has risen dramatically across the Arab and Muslim world. Increasingly negative public attitudes toward the United States and the perception that Washington no longer plays a peacemaking role are strongly influenced by this issue. The perpetuation of the conflict increasingly bedevils our ability to build alliances for other critical challenges facing the region, such as the situations in Iran and Iraq. It also fuels instability and violent conflict in neighboring arenas, such as Lebanon. Finally, the conflict complicates the campaign for social and political reform in Arab societies. Arab-Israeli peacemaking should be an integral part of the broader U.S. reform agenda. By pursuing a robust peace process, we also deny authoritarian leaders and militant oppositionists across the region an issue that they exploit frequently.

Arab and Israeli negotiators themselves have admitted time and again that outside help from the United States is required to help resolve the deep issues that divide them. Our involvement, which all sides continue to demand, is vital to improve the prospects for peace. Bush 41 and Clinton understood this and assigned it due importance. Their successes or failures aside, both administrations were widely seen in the region as committed to Arab-Israeli diplomacy, generating benefits for the United States in other realms, including cooperation in counterterrorism and containing Iran and Iraq. Bush 43 took a different approach, assigning a higher priority to other issues, including the war against Saddam and regime change in Iraq. Even before September 11, but particularly afterward, the administration heard from many corners about the damage caused by escalating Israeli-Palestinian violence and growing anxiety about a complete collapse of the peace process. Appeals to the Bush 43 administration from Saudi leaders have been well documented, but there were others in the region and in the U.S. government who warned against the corrosive effect on U.S. strategic interests of disengaging from active Arab-Israeli peacemaking.

The next administration and its diplomatic team must be prepared to give U.S. engagement in the Arab-Israeli peace process a high priority among our national interests. This is not charity work, nor a favor we do for the parties. The idea that the United States "cannot want peace more than the parties themselves" poses a false choice for policymakers, suggesting that the United States should be deeply involved only when the parties are ready and has no business being actively engaged when they are not. In the changed world after September 11 and in view of the worsening crisis in Iraq, the need to rebuild strong alliances and deepen cooperation with Arab states has grown exponentially. When the United States was engaged and was seen as engaged in the peace process, said a former senior official reflecting on the Clinton administration's efforts, "the corollary benefit for us was every Arab leader want(ed) to talk" about cooperation on other issues, including counterterrorism. The Arabs and Israelis need peace more than the United States does, but broader U.S. interests in the region require an active diplomatic search for peace as much as or more than the parties themselves do.

The study group recognizes that future administrations will have a range of foreign and domestic policy choices to make, and the unresolved and stalemated Arab-Israeli conflict is unlikely to appear attractive, tempting the United States to wait until the parties seem ready for active peacemaking. Given what we have heard from so many former policy officials and seen in recent years, this approach is guaranteed to fail. The conflict will not reverse course on its own and is likely to deteriorate further. In addition, as the Bush 43 years suggest, sitting on the sidelines is impossible anyway, given how deeply invested the United States is—politically, strategically, and economically—in the Arab-Israeli conflict and in the region as a whole.

The United States has the power and influence to stem the conflict's further deterioration, preserve the viability of endgame solutions, and explore whether openings for negotiations are possible. However, it requires strong and sustained commitment from the next president's administration. The president must demonstrate, in words and deeds, that the peace process is an important part of the administration's agenda and will remain so throughout his or her term in office.

Style and Substance

> *Our conceptions were … filtered far too much through what Israel needed and wanted and required.*
> —Former senior official, reflecting on U.S. diplomacy in the late 1990s

Lesson 2. U.S. policy must never be defined anywhere but in Washington. Consultations with the parties must take place and policy revisions based on those consultations are inevitable, but our policy must be seen as our own.

Arabs and Israelis have always sought to shape our policy and dictate our tactics. We should expect this behavior in the future as well, and there is nothing out of the ordinary about their efforts. But U.S. policy, as defined by the president, must always be seen and executed as our own doing. Even as we adjust our policy to changing circumstances, we cannot be seen to shift with pressures from one party or another or abandon negotiations at the first sign of distress, be it violence, political turmoil, or resistance from the parties. The Middle East is a tough neighborhood, and there will be many efforts to derail U.S. policy from both regional rejectionists and regional governments. In the face of these forces, our diplomacy must show toughness and resilience to be effective.

Bush 41's greatest achievement in the peace process—the 1991 Madrid peace conference—resulted from a clearly defined presidential priority, sustained diplomacy by Secretary of State Baker, full consultations with all parties, and U.S. determination during the negotiations' endgame to see its own policy through. The administration's approach to the process before the Madrid conference was surely influenced by the ebb and flow of diplomacy;

the outcome reflected what the parties could live with as much as what the United States wanted to achieve. However, the administration never lost sight of the minimum requirements for success, and it did not allow entreaties or pressures from the parties to shake its determination to produce a historic initiative that would serve U.S. interests and positively shape the larger strategic environment.

In contrast, at the Geneva summit in March 2000, without its own agenda to pursue, the United States was reduced to delivering an Israeli proposal to Syria with no substantive U.S. contribution. In fact, Israel waited until the last minute before delivering its talking points to Clinton, who felt compelled to deliver them even though the United States had no opportunity to massage them or to try to influence Israeli bottom lines. During the final push in 2000 on the Syrian track, Clinton and his team proved overly deferential to the domestic constraints that Prime Minister Barak argued were keeping him from closing a deal, weakening our position to mediate between the two contending parties.

During the Camp David II summit in July, there was much more back and forth between the United States and Israel than was the case in Geneva, but in the end Clinton acceded to Barak's request to blame Arafat publicly for the summit's failure. Both Arabs and Israelis understood that the summit had accomplished much in identifying the core issues to be negotiated. However, because of Barak's domestic political needs, the blame campaign against Arafat complicated the diplomatic follow-up and contradicted Clinton's own explicit assurances to the Palestinian leader and his team before Camp David (the question of summitry is explored further in Lesson 10). During the summit, the study group was repeatedly told, the United States gave the Palestinians proposals that originated with Israel. In the words of a senior U.S. policymaker, the Clinton team allowed itself to be manipulated and relinquished too much control over U.S. policy. Others shared this sentiment in describing the brief but eventful Clinton-Barak collaboration. However, throughout the Oslo years, Washington also tended to be too soft on Arafat and the Palestinian leadership when it came to incitement governance and public institutions. The trade-off between governance and progress in the negotiations, which ironically came at the urging of both Palestinians and Israelis (including Rabin), weakened the very process it was intended to sustain.

The Clinton years also reflect certain achievements. During Netanyahu's tenure as prime minister of Israel (1996–99), when it appeared that the process might collapse, the Clinton team worked hard to keep the process on track, first with the Hebron accord and later at Wye and after, even at the price of growing tension with the Israeli government. Clinton's personal involvement also evolved substantially over the years, demonstrating his administration's support for the peace process.

As with Clinton, during the Bush 43 years, there were moments when policy was shaped too much by parties outside Washington. The U.S. response to the direct and pointed Saudi appeal for U.S. intervention in 2001 reflected a reactive approach, suggesting that the catalyst for U.S. policy was coming from outside Washington. Later, the United States took far more dramatic steps that diverted attention away from U.S. diplomacy, as when the Washington-sponsored Roadmap initiative was effectively set aside in favor of Prime Minister Ariel Sharon's unilateral Gaza disengagement initiative. Washington essentially relinquished control of the process. "I did get calls [from Washington] being asked to help think through what should be—not the Israeli—but the U.S. policy or strategy," said an Israeli official about this period.

It would have been unwise, if not impossible, to oppose disengagement; after all, Sharon was promising to dismantle settlements and withdraw settlers from Gaza and the West Bank for the first time in history. Where Washington erred, especially after Mahmoud Abbas' election as Palestinian president, was in failing to link the Israeli plan to a revived political process in the region, which would have transformed a unilateral plan into an opportunity for sustained peacemaking. Officially, the need for such a diplomatic move was widely accepted throughout the administration, and there were a variety of ways to fuse the two initiatives, including a stronger West Bank component to the Gaza plan. But the United States backed off instead—the study group was told repeatedly—and ultimately abandoned even its own modest efforts to use the opening presented by the Israeli initiative to create new momentum in the peace process.

It is particularly important to avoid becoming diplomatically gun-shy in the face of politics in the region, a factor that traditionally relates more to Israeli than Arab politics. It is fair for an Israeli prime minister or Palestinian leader to argue for modified U.S. tactics because of their own domestic political constraints, but it is equally important for the United States not to accept such arguments at face value. Regional leaders can choose whether to participate in the peace process, and once they have chosen, it is they and not U.S. officials who must lead their domestic constituencies to support the policies. The stronger our representation in the region and the better our diplomatic reporting from our embassies, the better an administration can distinguish between real domestic political crises in the region and bargaining by regional leaders for favorable U.S. policy positions. During the run-up to disengagement, Sharon argued that he needed more U.S. support, even beyond the far-reaching April 2004 assurances on settlements and refugees, claiming that he did not have the votes in his cabinet to pass a disengagement resolution. Our diplomats knew this was not the case, and offered no further U.S. support; Sharon's cabinet passed the resolution.

The United States can and should support leaders who take risks for peace using diplomatic, economic, or security assurances, but we should also be careful not to grant too much influence to any party's domestic concerns. Bush 41 devoted too little attention to domestic politics in the region. Clinton devoted too much, often allowing Israeli domestic politics effectively to veto critical issues, most notably the question of settlements. The Bush 43 administration also proved overly deferential to the stated political problems of the Israeli government while tending to turn a blind eye toward domestic constraints on the Arab side.

> *You need to light a thousand candles out there and hope a couple of them stay on or work ... try to make a penetration at a lot of points instead of one, because ... it demonstrates momentum.*
> —**Former U.S. envoy**

Lesson 3. The United States must not only exploit openings but also actively encourage, seek out, and create opportunities for peacemaking.

Presidents normally do not need encouragement to be activists, as it was through a life of political activism that they rose to the highest office in the land. This activism—the urgency of creating, seeking, encouraging, and exploiting opportunities—is also indispensable for success in the peace process. Because a president has limited time available to launch initiatives and has competition from other priorities, Arab-Israeli diplomacy must be launched early and with a White House mandate to hit the ground running, stay involved, and constantly either look for openings or create them through agile diplomacy. Ideal conditions will not present themselves in the Middle East any more than they will appear elsewhere. "You don't get the fundamentals in place unless you have an active diplomacy to begin with," said a former official and senior diplomat.

Following a pattern first established by Nixon and Henry Kissinger, who generated diplomatic openings in the aftermath of the 1973 Arab-Israeli war, Bush 41 and Baker seized on international and regional strategic shifts to move the parties actively toward a defined objective. Out of the crisis created by the Iraqi occupation of Kuwait, the United States created an opportunity for peacemaking and successfully launched the Madrid peace process. Critically, Washington was active in seeking out opportunities rather than waiting for ideal conditions to present themselves.

The Clinton administration was actively engaged throughout its two terms, and at times sought to exploit opportunities. Clinton and his team leveraged Oslo to create an international donor process to aid Palestinians and initially to reinvigorate the multilateral negotiation track. Both elements were critical to facilitating and underwriting the process, providing the Palestinians with much-needed financial assistance and creating regional incentives for Israel. In addition, although the United States was only minimally involved in Jordanian-Israeli negotiations, its economic and political support cemented the peace treaty and strengthened King Hussein at home. But despite an intense level of activity, at certain critical junctures in Arab-Israeli negotiations, the Clinton administration failed effectively to create or exploit opportunities. Clinton laid out his boldest ideas for Israeli-Palestinian peace—the so-called Clinton parameters—much too late, in his final days in office, and in a manner that all but invited the next administration to back away from peacemaking.

As mentioned earlier, the administration also missed or mishandled two promising opportunities in Israeli-Syrian negotiations. The study group heard three different narratives—Israeli, Syrian, and American—about the failure of the Rabin deposit in 1993 and the abortive Shepherdstown and Geneva summits in 2000. Though these narratives conflicted, a consensus emerged that the Clinton administration repeatedly failed to capitalize on openings.[5] On balance, Clinton placed the right priority on Arab-Israeli peacemaking, but missteps in policy formulation and execution left a legacy of decidedly mixed results.

Bush 43 failed to exploit openings of a different sort during a far more tumultuous period. Bush 43 inherited the Palestinian Intifada and the failed Camp David II and Geneva summits, conditions far more detrimental than those that Clinton faced. But even so, throughout his administration, Bush 43 appeared to be uninterested in testing whether possible openings could be exploited to create diplomatic opportunities. In 2001, little was done even after both parties accepted the conclusions of the Sharm el-Sheikh fact-finding commission (the Mitchell report). In 2002, Washington largely aborted Secretary of State Colin Powell's diplomacy. With the 2003 Roadmap peace initiative came U.S. commitment to monitor implementation, but this commitment was soon abandoned, and in 2004, the Roadmap was set aside in deference to Israel's disengagement initiative. Perhaps most important, Mahmoud Abbas's accession to power in 2005 resulted in almost no change in the U.S. approach or policy. In 2002 and 2007, the administration greeted an Arab peace initiative—a potential paradigm shift from a 1948 to a 1967 mind-

---

5. According to one Israeli negotiator interviewed by the study group, "Rabin was utterly disappointed by the way [the deposit] was handled by the U.S. team … certainly Kissinger, probably also Baker, Holbrooke, that kind of negotiator who also knows bargaining would have said to Assad, 'You know, I was in Jerusalem the other day … and I may be able to get something from Rabin, but I need 'X,' and he would have gone back and forth five times …. But my sense immediately was that [Christopher] basically laid it on the table and Assad immediately started haggling." U.S., Israeli, and Syrian accounts differ. These contending narratives will be addressed in a subsequent study group publication.

set that signaled broader regional acceptance of Israel—with bare-
ly a lukewarm response, and failed to test whether there was a
major change in Arab attitudes toward peace with Israel.

In Arab-Israeli diplomacy, as with other conflicts, the United States has no choice but to deal with the leaders it encounters. When leaders are forward-leaning, it is easier for Washington to get behind them and generate additional momentum in
the peace process. When leaders are intransigent, U.S. negotiators
must seek out and create opportunities. Following Barak's election in 1999, the Clinton administration quickly understood that
a window of opportunity had opened and sought to capitalize
on the moment. But in doing so, Washington set aside far too
much of the received wisdom about peacemaking. Clinton and
his team not only embraced Barak's priorities, including the decision to put the Israeli-Palestinian track on hold, but also Barak's
tactics, as with the convening of summit meetings—at Israel's be-
hest—when the ground had not been adequately prepared. The
net result of these decisions was to cede effective control over U.S.
policy to the Israelis.

The administration failed to put its imprint on critical endgame negotiations on both the Palestinian-Israeli and Syrian-
Israeli tracks and to shape pivotal developments such as Israel's
withdrawal from south Lebanon in early 2000. The administration also did not use other regional partners effectively, relying first
on a Saudi channel to the Syrians, which proved wholly ineffec-
tive, and later in 2000 completely ignoring regional players such
as Egypt when Palestinian leaders needed wider Arab support for
concessions on core issues, a decision Clinton-era officials regret
in retrospect. Clinton himself also became overinvolved during
Barak's tenure, providing the Israeli leader virtually unfettered access, which effectively devalued the power of the presidency (see
Lesson 6). In the Arab-Israeli peace process, as in many enduring

conflicts, the leadership dimension is undoubtedly crucial, which is why Barak's ascendance and his prioritization of the peace process were so important. But the Clinton administration failed to exploit the opportunity presented to it. The United States also has tried mistakenly to cherry-pick Palestinian negotiating partners, sometimes seeking to bypass more senior figures whom Washington perceives as intransigent. This approach tends to backfire; when we try to pick our own winners, our diplomacy often loses. The study group was repeatedly told that this was the case at Camp David II in 2000, when U.S. negotiators selectively cultivated Palestinians considered to be more accommodating. The tendency continued throughout the Bush 43 years, with Washington's staunch support of figures like Mohammed Dahlan, even when he was not the designated interlocutor for the Palestinian leadership. A related problem for our security coordinators working with the PA was the lack of coherence and coordination within the U.S. government. Different agencies backed and financially supported different Palestinian security officials, often running at cross-purposes with the policies and preferences of the Palestinian leadership.

> *The issue is too important to our national interests not to push it towards resolution at this stage, and I think it's particularly unfortunate not to do so when the outlines of an agreement are so clear to virtually everyone.*
>
> **—Former senior National Security Council official**

> *If we had gotten more bottom lines, we could have conditioned Arab moderates.*
>
> **—Former Senior Clinton administration official**

LESSON 4. *The peace process has moved beyond incrementalism and must aim for endgame solutions. This not only requires U.S. leadership to help the parties make the necessary trade-offs on core issues, but also a commitment to an expanded diplomatic approach that involves key international and regional actors.*

The failure of the Oslo process and the demise of the Roadmap signal the end of incrementalism, the step-by-step diplomacy in Arab-Israeli negotiations by which the parties tried to negotiate interim agreements that would build confidence and momentum toward resolving the more difficult final settlement issues. As far back as the late 1970s, interim agreements have, by and large, not succeeded, and their failure has increased mistrust rather than built confidence. On both the Syrian and Palestinian tracks, the broad outlines of viable negotiated settlements are well known to all sides, and thus, the next president should eschew incrementalism and interim agreements in favor of an approach that concentrates the minds of the parties on the concessions necessary to end the conflict.

Although Clinton's Camp David II summit and the diplomacy that followed turned out to be costly setbacks for U.S. diplomacy, they did legitimize debate about a host of previously taboo subjects and directed the parties away from incremental solutions. But the Bush 43 administration was unwilling to continue the endgame diplomacy Clinton began in mid-2000, and throughout its two terms failed to use U.S. diplomacy to narrow the confines of the negotiations. Jettisoning gradualism does not mean that future agreements cannot be implemented over time, but it does suggest that the United States should aim for endgame solutions and help the parties make the necessary trade-offs to reach agreement on core issues. When the parties reach an impasse, Washington should not shy away from putting forward its own ideas. Without U.S. commitment, there is little hope for progress.

The broad outlines of possible trade-offs are well known, but it likely will fall on U.S. shoulders to develop the strategy and approach to introduce endgame solutions into the peace process.[6] If the past is prologue, the parties will encounter intractable issues that will require U.S. intervention and ideas. At the same time, events on the ground can weaken the viability of potential solutions—something Washington must seek to forestall.

The endgame challenge will be the most difficult aspect of peace process diplomacy for the president and the negotiating

6. While it is beyond the scope of the study group's mandate to recommend a detailed peace plan, it is not difficult to identify clear guidelines for a negotiated settlement that go beyond the general principles laid out in UN Security Council resolutions (i.e., 242, 338, 1397, etc.), but still leave enough detail for the parties to work out through negotiations. These guidelines—contained in documents like the Clinton parameters (2000; see Appendix), the Moratinos report on the Taba talks (2001), and especially the Nusseibeh-Ayalon initiative (2002)—cover the essential trade-offs required for a viable settlement, and polling in the region consistently shows a remarkable degree of majority support for them among both Israelis and Palestinians. Furthermore, they improve upon and are consistent with recent American initiatives, like the Roadmap and the Sharon-Bush letters.
• Two independent states—Israel and Palestine—using the June 1967 lines, with agreed adjustments, as the territorial basis for an end of the conflict.
• Palestinian refugees receive compensation, and have the right to return to the Palestinian state (including any areas "swapped" with Israel), repatriation to third countries, living in Israel (in cases where Israel agrees), or to remain where they are.
• Israeli settlers relocated, except those living in areas being "swapped."
• Arrangements for a shared Jerusalem that accommodate separate Israeli and Palestinian sovereignties while also protecting sites that Jews, Christians, and Muslims deem holy.
• Mutually agreed security arrangements, with rights, obligations, and limitations for both sides, as well as the presence of agreed-upon international peacekeeping forces.
   The outlines of an Israeli-Syrian peace treaty are also well-known, essentially following the land-for-peace model established by Israel and Egypt in 1979. The basic parameters were spelled out in the draft treaty discussed at Shepherdstown, with a range of details to be resolved through negotiations. See draft treaty in the Appendix.

team, for as well as the United States may define the issues, the U.S. approach could come under fire within the region and from domestic U.S. interest groups. Although the parties want Washington to be directly involved in reaching a settlement, they sometimes resist the United States mightily whenever it pushes in that direction. Much of this can be avoided through careful regional consultations before releasing a plan. At home, a strong case by the president about why peace process diplomacy serves U.S. interests and how it will open doors for Washington across the region can generate additional domestic support.

The United States has a new and valuable asset to leverage, namely, the possibility of enveloping American diplomacy in a regional context of Arab state support. As noted earlier, Bush 43 failed to respond twice when Arab states indicated a fundamental change in policy in 2002 and 2007 with the Saudi-backed Arab peace initiative. Future administrations must find a way to build on these new developments within Arab politics, not to compel Israeli acceptance of Arab policy, but to create a regional support structure for the hard decisions that Israel, the Palestinians, Syria, and Lebanon will need to make. Building a web of regional support is critical not only for insulating the process from rejectionist forces (e.g., Iran and its allies) but as a building block for pursuing U.S. interests in the Gulf and across the region.

Some will view regional support as inevitably coming at Israel's expense. In reality, the opposite is true. Bringing in critical regional players, such as Saudi Arabia, provides Israel with a wider process of normalization with the broader Arab and Muslim worlds, a goal Israeli leaders have long sought. On the Arab side, the study group was frequently reminded that Arab negotiators broadly accept Washington's special relationship with Israel; they do not expect the United States to jeopardize those ties and want Washington to capitalize on its influence, not squander it.

Bush 41 and Baker understood the importance of broad support for peacemaking and created a multilateral negotiating track after Madrid. Early on, Clinton showed his understanding of the same factor by supporting the regional economic summits that began at Casablanca. Later the multilateral track was allowed to wither and die. The Casablanca process ended in 1997, and a range of regional economic initiatives were quietly abandoned. The Clinton administration brought Arab leaders into the peace process, but at the pivotal moment decided to shut them out from Camp David, failing even to keep the Arabs briefed on developments, then desperately seeking their support when the process faltered.

In 2002, Bush 43 articulated a strong vision of peace that focused on general endgame solutions. But his endorsement of a two-state solution, which he repeated throughout both terms, was never fleshed out. Bush 43 and Powell did create the international Quartet—the United States, United Nations, European Union, and Russia—which has tremendous potential as a diplomatic tool. But the administration failed to leverage the combined clout of these outside actors into an effective stabilization effort or revived political process. The Bush 43 administration was perceived as failing to support Quartet envoys, such as James Wolfensohn; in November 2005, the administration tried to keep him out of the process at the very moment when his mission was at its make-or-break point.

At the end of his first term, Bush 43 made final status commitments to Israel in the context of disengagement without consulting meaningfully with other parties, which had the net impact of eroding Palestinian and Arab trust. U.S. assurances to Israel were offered to support a unilateral move rather than a negotiated or even coordinated process, breaking with long-established patterns of U.S. diplomacy. Even so, adept diplomacy could have linked the initiative to a political process that benefited both sides. An otherwise reasonable and shrewd diplomatic move to help Sharon politically, the Bush 43 assurances failed to achieve the more important objective of having a lasting and positive effect on the political track.

> *Why negotiate all these details, and in such a painstaking way, if there's really no cost for violation in the implementation phase? Then what integrity do the agreements have?*
> —**Leading analyst**

LESSON 5. Commitments made by the parties and agreements entered into must be respected and implemented. The United States must ensure compliance through monitoring, setting standards of accountability, reporting violations fairly to the parties, and exacting consequences when commitments are broken or agreements not implemented.

The diplomatic process itself should not be valued over results, which remain the ultimate indicator of progress toward peace. From the Bush 41 administration to the present, the United States failed to monitor performance and enforce commitments the parties made to each other and to Washington; this failure was highlighted more than any other issue throughout the study group's consultations. Former policymakers widely acknowledged that the lack of accountability was corrosive, eroding confidence among the parties, undermining U.S. standing, and allowing destructive developments to proceed unchecked.

The Oslo process lacked systems of effective monitoring and dispute resolution, and the United States did not step into the breach. From the outset, the parties held deeply divergent inter-pretations of the agreements, but U.S. officials only occasionally intervened to define the parties' obligations precisely. Officials in-terviewed by the study group understood well the problems that undermined the credibility of the process during this period: Pal-estinian violence that contravened the PLO's commitment to end violence and terrorism; incitement from many quarters that undermined the mutual recognition spelled out in Oslo; corrup-tion that undercut Palestinian efforts to develop the governmental infrastructure to sustain independence; large numbers of Israeli checkpoints and roadblocks that, while enhancing Israeli security, blocked Palestinian transportation and economic links; Israeli set-tlement expansion, which, while not explicitly barred under Oslo, was understood by all sides to destroy confidence in the viability of a process designed to transfer West Bank and Gaza territory to Palestinians; and Israeli delays and refusals to complete agreed-upon withdrawals from territory.

The same applied to PA inaction in collecting and control-ling illegal arms throughout the Oslo period: Though the PA was subject to painstakingly negotiated provisions, there was little sys-tematic effort to assess compliance and adjust our policy on the basis of performance. Once the Intifada erupted in 2000, it was too late, as Palestinians turned their arsenals against Israelis. An-other example was the Clinton administration's inaction in the face of Prime Minister Barak's turnabout over transferring con-trol of three Palestinian villages near Jerusalem. The Israeli move undermined Palestinian public support and severely eroded trust between the negotiating teams. As was often the case, U.S. poli-cy folded in the face of presumed Israeli domestic constraints—a judgment that took little or no account of Palestinian needs or the larger impact of tolerating a pattern of blatant disregard for signed commitments.

The need to "keep the process alive," which became the mantra throughout the Oslo years, was deemed more important than having the United States take strong positions when the parties did not comply with commitments and agreements. There were exceptions, such as the diplomacy surrounding the Hebron accord in 1997 or the implementation of the Wye agreement in 1998, when the Clinton administration singled out the Netanyahu government for noncompliance. But these episodes were exceptions to the rule. In retrospect, the trade-off between expediency and compliance was dangerous and often unnecessary, and future U.S. negotiators should take a different approach.

In addition to the U.S. failure to hold the parties accountable to each other, the United States also failed to ensure compliance to commitments made to Washington. Two of the most striking examples were the Israeli commitment, made orally in 2003 and in writing in 2004, to dismantle settlement outposts set up under Prime Minister Sharon. The Sharon government did not dismantle the outposts, and the Bush 43 administration did nothing in response.

Similarly, the U.S.-brokered Agreement on Movement and Access (November 2005) for Gaza—which Washington viewed as central to the success of Israeli disengagement—began to crumble even before the ink was dry. The agreement intended to ensure that Gaza remained accessible to the West Bank, the outside world, and Israel, so that Israeli withdrawal would not lead to siege-like conditions for the area's 1.5 million Palestinians. With Secretary of State Rice having gone out on a limb to mediate the accord down to the minutest detail, itself a questionable use of U.S. negotiating prowess, walking away afterward only further conditioned the parties to view such agreements as anything but solemn.

There are times when monitoring missions need to be based in the region and have personnel assigned to observe the activities of the parties on a full-time basis. Issues develop, sometimes daily, and an intense, hands-on manager needs to be on the spot to deal with problems as they arise and keep the parties focused on a common goal rather than the day's headlines. "[We] need to establish an office there," a former envoy told the study group, adding that Washington would be best served by "a permanent mediation officer, [in] bad times or good times, [with a] political, economic, monitoring, security component. It's too big an elephant ... to try to take a special envoy zero to sixty into final status issues." A U.S. team also needs to work closely with other international actors, such as the European Union, the United Nations, and the World Bank, which have large, semipermanent missions in place in the region.

But the lesson about monitoring and verification has never been learned. The Mitchell report, the Roadmap, and disengagement all would have benefited from a concerted, committed, and engaged monitoring effort. When the United States has tried its hand at compliance, as with the Clinton effort post-Wye—especially on security cooperation—meaningful results have been accomplished. As part of the Annapolis process the Bush 43 administration signalled its renewed interest in monitoring, although the scope of the U.S. role remained uncertain.

The study group is mindful that policy implementation, even of agreements, is not an exact science. It influenced by local politics, changes in the negotiating environment, and even U.S. domestic politics. Certain trade-offs are inescapable. But without an effective third-party monitoring and dispute-resolution mechanism, and without third-party determination and political will to call it like it is and enforce commitments and agreements, those same commitments and agreements become worthless and the fundamental trust needed to advance negotiations is undermined. The one U.S. effort to formally monitor an agreement, the post-Aqaba monitoring mission in 2003, was aborted after less than three months and never reported violations by the parties.

The Foreign Policy Process and U.S. Domestic Politics

> *There's no substitute … for the direct participation of the president of the United States. Whether we've spoiled the parties or not … it doesn't matter. They're spoiled now. They expect the president of the United States to be there.*

—**Former White House official**

> *We devalue the president's assets by using him too much.*

—**Former White House official**

LESSON 6. *The direct intervention of the president is vital, but presidential assets are finite and should be used selectively and carefully. Too direct a role runs the risk of devaluing the power of the office. Too modest a role runs the other risk of failing to capitalize on diplomatic openings.*

Presidential assets in the form of direct presidential intervention are finite and should be held in reserve for pivotal moments when such intervention is both necessary and useful. Arabs and Israelis have grown accustomed to direct presidential involvement, which can be crucial to closing a deal, but it is essential that the president not be drawn in too early or become too accessible during the early phases of a negotiation, when issues are best left to senior aides and members of the administration. In earlier periods, the direct involvement of presidents Nixon, Ford, and Carter, all of whom helped lead important negotiations and conclude pathbreaking Arab-Israeli agreements, is instructive in its careful calibration of purpose, process, timing, and the selective use of presidential assets.

Bush 41 defined the goals he wanted to achieve and delegated day-to-day responsibility to Secretary Baker. The president remained engaged, exchanging periodic phone calls and messages with leaders and having discussions during their visits to Washington, but at no time did Bush 41 himself become the chief negotiator. He did not need to intervene directly to close the deal to launch the Madrid conference.

Clinton established peace as a priority of his administration, and Secretary Christopher appointed a special coordinator to handle the day-to-day process. Clinton himself remained largely aloof for almost six years, though he engaged directly when called upon, as in an early summit with Syrian President Assad; in phone calls, messages, and visits with regional leaders; and last-minute problem solving before signing ceremonies.

The president's personal engagement in the process increased at the Wye summit in late 1998, when White House intervention and U.S. arbitration successfully prevented the Oslo process from collapsing. Part of the price of reaching the Wye accord was the promise of a first-ever presidential visit to the Palestinian areas as well as Israel, which Clinton deftly used to coax and prod both sides to adhere to Wye. The visit itself was used judiciously and focused on keeping Wye and the larger process on track.

But in late 1999 and 2000, the president became overly involved, and presidential assets were misused and devalued. Clinton's penchant for telephone diplomacy and an open door to the Oval Office were just two signs of how the president was quickly becoming the "action officer" for the peace process. "I don't know anyone … who would disagree that the president was overused," said a member of the Clinton team; "the power of the presidency was devalued." In particular, Clinton's willingness to take every phone call from Prime Minister Barak—at times on an almost daily basis, the study group was told—devalued the president's latent power and denied Clinton the critical distance that a president often must have when dealing with detailed and nuanced policy problems.

The problem was not only the lack of selectivity but also the misapplication of presidential assets, as when Clinton presented his parameters to Israelis and Palestinians in late December 2000. Clinton sought to influence the parties with the proviso that the proposal would expire when his term ended the next month. The desire to inject urgency into the last-ditch talks is understandable, but by preemptively declaring that the proposal would soon expire and that it therefore did not represent a definitive change in U.S. policy, Clinton undercut his own initiative. The tactic seemed to invite the parties to bide their time and respond to Clinton with conditions that effectively gutted the parameters. The move gave Bush 43 even more of an excuse to step away from active mediation.

Bush 43 largely opted out of Arab-Israeli peacemaking. Whether it was due to a lack of interest in wading too deep into the role of mediator or because the issue was assigned a lower priority in the administration's strategic assessment, for most of his two terms, Bush 43 kept a studied distance from Arab-Israeli negotiations. He also shied away from fully investing a subordinate with real responsibility or direction to advance the peace process, whether it was the secretary of state or any of the envoys who were sent to the region.

In 2002, Bush 43 sent Secretary Powell to the region to deal with a surge in Palestinian terrorism and Israel's reoccupation of Palestinian cities. However, Powell's mission was beset by Washington in-fighting that undercut his ability to arrange even an interim deal and thereby walk the parties back from the brink. Throughout Bush 43's second term, as the crisis in Iraq worsened, the administration continued to maintain a low diplomatic profile on the Arab-Israeli conflict, despite bipartisan sentiment outside the White House—as reflected in the *Iraq Study Group Report* (December 2006)—that reviving the peace process should be part of an overall strategy to revive U.S. influence, bolster moderate forces in the region, and stabilize the situation in Iraq.

The right balance of intervention versus restraint can and must be struck, and in this sense, the current lesson converges with previous lessons. The president needs to set broad strategic objectives early in the administration, establish the Arab-Israeli conflict as a priority, empower a team with real diplomatic clout, and ensure that the effort operates well under strong leadership. The president also needs to be actively involved in promoting the strategy to the parties, the U.S. public, and the international community.

The presidential "clock" is a critical factor in deciding if, when, or how a president should intervene personally in the Arab-Israeli peace process. As important as peacemaking is, there is only so much usable presidential time to devote to it. Given the U.S. electoral calendar, by late in the third year of a term, time is running short for new initiatives. Bush 41 exploited the opening provided by the 1991 Gulf War to devise a strategy for a peace process breakthrough. Given the very favorable conditions that Clinton inherited, he and his team waited far too long before moving the parties toward a possible endgame. By the time Clinton convened make-or-break summit meetings in 2000, the parties had developed bad habits that weakened the foundations of what had been a promising opportunity for peace. The Bush 43 administration's initiative in 2007 to organize a major international meeting and support renewed Israeli-Palestinian talks also came very late, after some parties had already resigned themselves to wait for the next U.S. administration.

> *If the top advisers don't have [expertise and cultural understanding], then ... the secretary of state or the president is not going to be given the full deck of cards.*
> —**Former senior official**
>
> *It was one of the most dysfunctional groups of people I've ever worked with and will ever work with.*
> —**Former State Department official, discussing the Clinton peace team**

LESSON 7. Build a diverse and experienced negotiating team steeped in regional and functional expertise; encourage open debate and collaboration within the government. A dysfunctional policy process should not be tolerated.

U.S. policymakers repeatedly stressed to the study group six elements of organizational success: clear lines of authority; a disciplined, diverse, and experienced team; debate; deliberation; information sharing; and proper policy planning and preparation. For much of the period under review, however, many of these elements were lacking.

Bush 41, under the policy management of Secretary Baker, incorporated most of the above elements. Baker assembled a diverse and experienced team that combined functional expertise with in-depth knowledge of Arabs and Israelis. U.S. ambassadors were integral members of his team and were used to maintain communications with key regional leaders, report and analyze events, and close gaps of perception or understanding in cross-cultural negotiations. Debate was encouraged and confidentiality maintained. Intensive preparation went into every aspect of negotiations, including Baker's eight shuttle missions between March and October 1991. Careful records were kept and the decision-making process was documented in an orderly manner. The administration's success also derived from the extraordinarily close relationship between the president and the secretary of state—admittedly unique in modern U.S. history—but even that relationship was marked by enough vibrancy and disagreement to assure that policy did not emerge as a homogenized shade of gray.

Clinton's secretaries of state, Warren Christopher and Madeleine Albright, assigned day-to-day responsibility for the peace process to a special Middle East coordinator. The peace team assembled during much of the administration had superior expertise regarding Israel, but far less expertise and experience in dealing with the Arabs. Assistant secretaries and ambassadors in the field often felt cut off from policy formulation and, at key junctures, did not participate in important diplomatic talks.

A wide range of interviewees told the study group that the Clinton peace team was too insular and largely cut off from traditional State Department and interagency support structures. "Policy was more run out of a back pocket," said a former official. Information was not shared, analysis and field reporting were often ignored, and insufficient written and analytical preparation preceded certain pivotal negotiations, such as Camp David II.

Still, the Clinton team was "lean" and streamlined, enjoying the confidence of policymakers, including the president. There was a high degree of personal rapport, which some former officials regarded as a major plus. But "dysfunctional" attributes of the policy process—as acknowledged by Clinton administration officials—were ultimately a drag on U.S. diplomacy. The Clinton team could have benefited from greater regional and cross-cultural expertise. The lack of cross-cultural negotiating skills was so acute toward the end of the Clinton period that the State Department's top Arabic translator, a talented and well-connected individual, was drafted into sensitive diplomatic dealings with senior Arab officials. The decision seemed based on expediency and a sudden awareness that the absence of Arab expertise was handicapping U.S. diplomacy.

The last-ditch talks regarding Jerusalem at Camp David also revealed a lack of knowledge about Arab culture. "There was no expert on our team on Islam or on Muslim perspectives," said a former Clinton administration official, "[so] when it came to dealing with Jerusalem, there's some very embarrassing episodes that betrayed our lack of knowledge or bias." A leading Arab diplomat told the study group that U.S. negotiators might have been surprised to learn that even conservative Arab views on Jerusalem were not too far off from Jewish perspectives. "The Haram and Al-Aqsa" are sacred for Muslims, he said; "everything else is real estate." More broadly, there was a general problem with preparation for Camp David II and the intensive diplomacy that followed, a legacy of the longer-term failure to use the years after Oslo to prepare detailed U.S. briefs on the key issues.

At Camp David there was no clear strategy for achieving results once the talks began, and precious little internal consensus about the core issues. "We could not stick with a strategy for more than twelve hours," said one U.S. negotiator. Important Arab state actors, left in the dark about U.S. policy, were unwilling or unable to assist our diplomacy at critical moments. The United States even shifted around its own team during the summit, signaling disarray to the parties.

There were also breakdowns in process under Bush 43, but of a different nature. It was often not clear who spoke for the president. Secretary Powell was undermined from within, damaging his influence over the parties. The National Security Council (NSC) often assumed an operational role, working largely through a back channel with Israel. NSC activities led to important understandings about a wide range of central issues, including the route of the Israeli separation barrier. There was little internal debate within the administration before making major policy decisions, as with the Sharon-Bush exchange of letters in 2004 on Israeli disengagement, an initiative that several senior officials criticized for unnecessarily weakening the U.S. negotiating position.[7]

Competition behind the scenes within the administration was so intense that there were even breakdowns in the normal record-keeping process. The study group was repeatedly told that careful records were not always maintained and shared in the Clinton and Bush 43 administrations. Seemingly routine and dull, accurate and durable record keeping is a prerequisite for managing a complex negotiating process with numerous moving parts. It is also one of the few elements of continuity in our foreign policy system, in which top personnel change from one administration to the next and diplomacy is often dated from inauguration day rather than accruing over time.

Meticulous record keeping is particularly vital to the Arab-Israeli conflict because the parties themselves—especially Israel—do so zealously. U.S. negotiators cannot afford to be caught off guard when prior understandings or agreements resurface or are reinterpreted years later as the parties seek advantage in the process. The president and secretary of state need not become bureaucratic watchdogs, but the success of an administration's policies can hinge on running a tight ship and marshaling and refining the bureaucracy's participation in the president's initiatives.

---

7. See the Appendix for the text of the letters.

*Meet with everyone, but don't take guidance from any-
one. You need to know when to push back. Jewish-
Americans and Arab-Americans are not monolithic.*
—Former secretary of state

LESSON 8. Build broad and bipartisan domestic support and
use political capital before it is too late in a presidential
term. Keep Congress well informed. Cultivate close relations on Capitol Hill and with advocacy communities without
being held captive to the agendas of domestic groups.

As with any high-profile policy, foreign or domestic, successful Arab-Israeli peacemaking requires a strong bipartisan coalition, with support from interest groups and Congress. U.S.
policymakers face an intense and varied array of concerned
parties at home, which is why bipartisanship is so essential.
But in the years since Madrid, the level of domestic partisan
acrimony has grown steadily, complicating a range of foreign
policy initiatives, including Middle East peacemaking.

Congressional action on Arab-Israeli relations tends to fall
into two broad categories: expressive measures, such as cosigned
letters, floor statements, and nonbinding resolutions; and legislation on foreign aid and arms sales. Expressive actions, though
not binding, send signals to U.S. policymakers and the parties in
the Middle East. Such action may not directly affect day-to-day
peacemaking, but it is a significant aspect of the larger political
environment in which Middle East diplomacy is conducted.

Given Congress' power of the purse, binding legislation on foreign aid—a prominent diplomatic tool in the region—has long
been the principal method by which Capitol Hill puts its stamp
on the peace process. Major arms sales and security assistance
packages, which require congressional approval, are also impor-

tant components of U.S. diplomacy and are closely watched by advocacy groups, the military, and other actors in the region. To ensure that economic and security assistance packages are tightly coordinated with our diplomacy, early and extensive consultation between the executive branch and Congress is required. Israeli advocacy groups, with or without the support of Israeli leaders, sometimes seek congressional support to shape the current administration's policy—or in some cases, to circumvent the executive branch or force an administration's hand on a controversial subject, as was the case with Jerusalem policy and the long-running controversy about whether to move the U.S. embassy, as well as Washington's relations with the PLO and the PA, to take just two examples from the post-Madrid period.

Cultivating close relations with Congress benefits U.S. negotiators. Keeping key members from both parties well briefed on U.S. strategy as it develops and gaining their confidence is vital, but often overlooked. More than with most foreign policy issues, a proactive strategy is required. There is no general rule for how an administration should respond to congressional action on Arab-Israeli issues; the choice to engage in a policy review, alter policy, or stay the course needs to be made on a case-by-case basis. That said, the more an administration invests in actively and eagerly cultivating congressional support, the lower the probability that domestic politics will constrain our negotiators, or that the parties will gain advantage from differences of opinion inside the Beltway.

A consistent theme that emerged in the study group's consultations is that domestic politics do not play the central role that is often ascribed to them. Without a doubt, they are influential, but they are far from determining. As our consultations made clear, presidential leadership is the most decisive factor. When presidents lead in Arab-Israeli diplomacy, Congress and public opinion follow; as legislators from both parties told the study group,

Congress especially will line up behind a president, provided the administration's strategy is sound and Israel's security is protected. But this truism is sometimes lost even among U.S. negotiators as the so-called anticipatory reflex sets in and policy choices are pre-emptively constrained. At times, U.S. policy on settlements and Jerusalem has reflected this phenomenon.

Arab-Israeli diplomacy is closely scrutinized, and it is all too easy for policymakers to buy into interest groups' false dichotomies of labeling leaders as friendly or not friendly toward Israel. Strong support for Israel has defined both Democrats and Republicans for many years, and is not a subject of debate between the major political parties. No president since 1967 has questioned Israel's vital security needs. All presidents have ensured that Israel receives the political and material support it needs to defend itself. The question has been whether a president has been willing to push back on political and economic matters involving Israel that do not directly relate to security, and the peace process thus tends to test the limits of presidential responsibility for foreign policy in the face of strong domestic interest groups.

For U.S. negotiators, cultivating a strong coalition of domestic support goes hand in hand with an astute appreciation of how vital it is for Israeli leaders to avoid tension with Washington. Among leading political parties and personalities in Israel, from which U.S. advocates for Israel draw inspiration, avoiding friction with Washington has become axiomatic, especially given the Shamir and Netanyahu legacies. This is a key source of leverage and influence for Washington that should not be overlooked or understated.

Bush 41 took a determined stance against Israeli settlement expansion, openly opposing Shamir. Initially, the dispute arose over Israel's request for economic assistance to relocate Soviet immigrants and the Shamir government's refusal to limit resettlement to Israel within the 1967 lines. Later, in 1991 and 1992, the United States conditioned an even larger Israeli request of $10 billion in loan guarantees on a complete freeze on settlements. The U.S. position was tough and determined, but more important, it focused exclusively on an issue that was discretionary for Israeli leaders rather than a security imperative.

In contrast, both Clinton and Bush 43 failed to argue strongly against Israeli policies or practices that were largely unrelated to security but contradicted U.S. policies or interests, such as settlement expansion and certain occupation practices. Undeniably, U.S. policy positions on these issues have eroded over time, even as they have become more controversial in Israel. The challenge for a president to engage in tough love with Israel—that is, support Israel's legitimate security requirements but not elective Israeli policies that may help a leader at home but contradict U.S. interests—is formidable, but it is also necessary if progress is to be achieved.

Clinton amassed substantial political capital at home. At times, he used it effectively, as with Netanyahu's failure to move forward with the Interim Agreement and later with his failure to comply with the Wye River accord. But Clinton's most ambitious attempt to tap into this vast reservoir of political capital came too late, when U.S. diplomacy was already hobbled for other reasons set forth in this study.

Bush 43 may have accumulated even more domestic political capital toward Israel, but he failed to use it. In March 2002, Bush 43 demanded publicly that Israel pull back from Palestinian cities it had reoccupied, but then dropped the demand and soon after called Sharon a "man of peace." Later, in 2004 and 2005, Bush allowed Sharon to dictate the scope of Gaza disengagement, failing to draw a strong enough connection to the West Bank to withstand charges that disengagement was little more than Israel's ridding itself of the burden of Gaza.

U.S. negotiators surely need to pay close attention to building domestic support, but they must also be careful not to let it dictate policy. The array of interest groups is sufficiently diverse, including within the broad pro-Israel community, that policymakers can build winning political coalitions to support their peace initiatives.

The Negotiator's Toolkit

It's critical to have a focal point to ensure that you create an investment. Administrations have to feel, and the people in the region have to feel, that we actually are invested. That means (an envoy) has to be visible. There's no such thing as having an invisible envoy.
—**Former senior official**

The credibility of the envoy is critical to the region. The region only wants to know one thing: Is this human being talking to the president of the United States directly?
—**Former cabinet official**

LESSON 9. A successful envoy needs the strong and unambiguous support of the White House, credibility with all parties, and a broad mandate. Envoys should not substitute for meaningful diplomacy. Better a policy without an envoy than an envoy without a policy.

The debate about when and how to use envoys has often substituted for serious policy deliberation. Too often, the first response to a problem in the region has been to send an envoy, as though the mere presence of another U.S. interlocutor will calm tempers. Equally often, the calls for an envoy are uncoupled from any suggestions as to what substantive policy steps should be taken—what, in short, the envoy should do. If the president lays out clear objectives, a diplomatic strategy, and a sound policy process, the envoy question will sort itself out.

Envoys are necessary stand-ins for the president or the secretary of state particularly at times when the latter does not take a leading role, as leaders cannot always afford to devote themselves exclusively to one issue for an extended period of time. In addition, given the highly complex nature of Arab-Israeli negotiations, envoys can be useful for their expertise and ability to manage a complicated negotiating process. Envoys are also critical in providing a focal point, not only for the parties, but also for the many offices and agencies within the U.S. government that have a role in the peace process. In an era of multilateral mediation, an envoy is also an important focal point for coordinating and sometimes imposing discipline on other third-party mediators. The more political clout an envoy carries, the more easily the envoy can serve as that focal point and the less need to have in-depth expertise, which senior advisers can provide.

If a serious monitoring effort is to be undertaken, an envoy should lead it, even if it requires extended stays in the region. The lack of a strong envoy based in the region and with a broad mandate was a major hindrance to transforming Israeli disengagement into a positive and stabilizing force. Last, envoys can be invaluable as generators of new thinking and fresh ideas, particularly when the process stalls, as it did in the mid-1990s, or falls apart completely, as it did in late 2000. When Israelis and Palestinians seemed unable to conclude the talks on the Oslo II interim agreement (1995), or when the process stalled over Hebron (1996 and 1997), U.S. envoys brought in creative ideas that allowed those negotiations to move toward conclusion.

Bush 41 empowered Secretary Baker as envoy, and the successes of his approach have been analyzed above. Baker's linking of a new Israeli aid request to a settlements freeze led to a crisis of confidence with the Shamir government. Although Baker could have done more to build confidence with the Shamir government and Israel advocacy groups at home, he was always careful to maintain credibility with the Israeli public, and toward the end of its term, the Bush 41 administration began to develop a close working relationship with the Rabin government.

The study group heard praise for the Clinton administration's decision to appoint a full-time coordinator to the Arab-Israeli conflict, but also heard an equal number of questions as to why Secretary Christopher and Secretary Albright did not play a more significant role. The study group also heard quite specific complaints about Clinton's peace team, including from Arab negotiators, regarding bias toward Israel and a lack of equal attention paid to Arab interests and political dynamics. "The perception always was that Dennis [Ross] started from the Israeli bottom line," said a prominent Arab negotiator, "that he listened to what Israel wanted and then tried to sell it to the Arabs.... He was never looked at ... as a trusted world figure or as an honest broker." "By the end, the Palestinians didn't fully trust Dennis," said a senior Clinton administration figure; "they thought he was tilted too much towards the Israelis." "We never felt that the American team was playing a fair game," said a senior Palestinian negotiator; "we always felt that there ... [was a] division of labor between the Israeli and the American teams.... The Israelis ... were using some Americans as a vanguard ... to explore our positions and to see to what extent we are ready to compromise or to concede." The study group heard similar views about officials in the Bush 43 White House. A successful envoy needs to be viewed as credible by all sides.

Elements of Success

Success requires total support from the White House, trust and credibility with the parties, a broad mandate, negotiating experience, and political clout.

White House Blessing. Whatever his standing among other negotiators, as Clinton's envoy, Ross clearly had administration support at almost every stage of his long tenure at the helm of U.S. peacemaking efforts. This support was an important source of strength for his mediation. The parties perceived Ross as having what one former cabinet official described as walk-in rights to the Oval Office.

Other envoys have not enjoyed the same levels of support. Anthony Zinni and James Wolfensohn did not always have the full backing of the Bush 43 White House, which made it difficult for them to be effective. "They're not backed up by anything," said a former senior administration figure about the Bush 43 envoys; "it's almost as much public relations as it is substance." The parties are supremely attuned to such signals. If they believe there is any lack of support from Washington for the envoy, as was the case when Wolfensohn tried to resolve the problem of movement of people and goods in and out of Gaza, the envoy's influence can be significantly undermined.

Expertise and Political Clout. Envoys do not need to be steeped in the intricacies of Arab-Israeli relations and carry political clout at the same time, but they do need to score high in at least one category. Arabs and Israelis have become accustomed to dealing with either high-profile interlocutors or highly experienced ones. Zinni compensated for lack of specific experience in the Arab-Israeli conflict with broad experience in the Arab world and his weight as a senior, well-respected military figure. Senator George Mitchell compensated for his relative lack of experience by bringing a substantial amount of stature to the process. In contrast, John Wolf, who lacked both political clout and extensive expertise with Arabs and Israelis, was not taken seriously by the parties.

However, scoring high in one or both categories is not a guarantee of success. As a former World Bank president, James Wolfensohn commanded the attention and respect of the parties, key international actors, Congress, and the U.S. government. But ultimately his mission failed due to a circumscribed mandate and lack of support from Washington (see above and in Lesson 4).

Former British Prime Minister Tony Blair, who began work as a Quartet envoy in July 2007, brought even greater stature to the role. The Blair mission was unique in both the prominence of the envoy and Washington's willingness to anoint a non-American. Early indications suggest that U.S. reluctance to cede too much control in the diplomatic process to a European may leave Blair with a circumscribed mandate. That said, Blair's stature as a world leader, his close bonds with Bush 43, his determination to gain Israel's trust, and his commitment to the peace process could make the critical difference between his mission and the pattern of failed envoys in recent years.

Finally, if an envoy's mission gathers momentum, the need for specialized expertise grows. The team around the envoy needs to have regional and cross-cultural skills, legal expertise, security and intelligence training, and economic and business know-how. When the United States mediated Israeli-Egyptian peace in the 1970s, the U.S. team was diverse and negotiators had a variety of backgrounds. Secretary Baker also could rely on a diverse team, including individuals with cross-cultural experience. He paid particular attention to input from U.S. ambassadors in the field. Later administrations fell short of this standard.

Full Menu. Successful Arab-Israeli peacemaking requires that an envoy be given a broad mandate that covers a range of key issues, including political, economic, and security matters. Under the Bush 43 administration, there was a tendency to divide portfolios and empower functional envoys. George Tenet, the director of the Central Intelligence Agency (CIA), was charged in 2001 with restoring security cooperation. Later, James Wolfensohn was given the economic file regarding Israel's disengagement initiative. Generals William Ward, Keith Dayton, and James Jones have served as security coordinators, but without any mandate to deal with the political process, which tends to define the relevance of any initiative. The Bush 43 pattern of dividing the traditional envoy into discrete, functional roles has not proven very successful; it has put our envoys in a position of mediating with one hand—sometimes both hands—tied behind their backs. The success of the current Blair mission hinges on whether the former prime minister can carve out a wide mandate and still maintain the support of the Bush 43 administration.

Symbols Matter. In Arab-Israeli peacemaking, as with most diplomatic missions, symbols can easily become substance. Each party is sensitive to the time and attention it receives from the mediator, often correlating it with trust. Attentive public and political classes are similarly attuned and can easily pounce on any and all signals that might suggest which way an envoy is leaning. This extends to something as mundane as travel itineraries and the question of where diplomatic shuttles are based. Envoys should avoid basing regional diplomatic missions in any one location, such as the practice since the mid-1990s of basing in Jerusalem. Arriving—whether by plane or car—and then departing in the course of a few hours, as was typically the case when visiting with Arab leaders, sends the wrong signal. A constant presence in the region can be accomplished without creating unneeded impressions of favoritism.

> *The thinking was that money and economics could sus-*
> *tain the process, [but] this was a huge mistake.*
> —**Senior Palestinian official**

LESSON 10. Use the diplomatic toolbox judiciously and pay close attention to developments on the ground. Tools, such as economic assistance and summitry, should be used with strategic objectives in mind, not merely to buy time.

During the nearly four decades of active U.S. engagement in the Arab-Israeli peace process, we have used an impressive array of diplomatic tools. However, from the Bush 41 administration to the present, the U.S. diplomatic toolbox was not used as effectively as it might have been. As this book emphasizes throughout, good policy starts with strong and focused leadership—a president willing and able to define priorities, organize an active diplomatic effort, and encourage follow-through with experienced and expert staff. Every president stamps a personal mark on the policy process, but certain characteristics and elements endure.

The creative diplomacy called for in this study requires the judicious use of both carrots and sticks in our foreign policy toolbox. U.S. economic and security assistance has been of crucial importance at key junctures in the peace process. Since the late 1970s, the United States has provided billions of dollars of aid to Israel and Egypt, not only as a reward for making peace but also to assure that Israel has the support it needs to take prudent risks in peace process diplomacy. U.S. diplomats have used other tools, such as international conferences, summitry, shuttle diplomacy, security guarantees, side letters, and written assurances, and threats and other punitive measures, as the need has arisen. As a great power, the United States traditionally has been mindful of the extraordinary weight that its diplomacy carries, but also of the sensitivity with which U.S. diplomatic tools must be employed.

Good information and intelligence should carry a high value, and thus, the role of professionals within government who collect, report, and analyze information is critical. Such professionals also offer a measure of continuity as senior officials come and go.

It is a well-known axiom in the intelligence community that most of what we know comes from open sources and diplomatic reporting. There is no substitute for recruiting the best officers to report and analyze issues in the peace process. There is tremendous value in using our senior diplomats in the field and a cross-section of sources on all sides to gain an accurate picture of developments on the ground and across the region. This is particularly important on the Israeli-Palestinian track, where day-to-day events can powerfully shape the negotiating environment. In both the Clinton and Bush 43 administrations, it appears that reporting and analysis from the field were not accorded high priority, whereas too much weight was assigned to information gleaned from phone calls between officials in the region and in Washington.

Nontraditional Diplomacy

Keeping abreast of developments and identifying emerging trends, within Israel, the Palestinian areas, and Arab societies more broadly, also requires investing in nontraditional diplomacy. Aside from the typical track II objectives of building informal networks across conflict divides and developing and floating new ideas, unofficial diplomacy is also an invaluable resource to test prevailing conventional wisdom and discreetly tap into outside expertise that may not be readily accessible in Washington. For negotiators, nontraditional diplomacy also helps to address opposition to formal negotiations and peacemaking, providing a venue to better understand and engage with opponents and, ideally, identify new actors from all sides who are willing to join the negotiations and the political process. Finally, at both the elite (track II dialogue) and popular (people-to-people) levels, nontraditional diplomacy humanizes the contending parties.

Not all such efforts need remain discreet. Certain initiatives, such as the Ayalon-Nusseibeh principles, can help to sustain and build popular support for peacemaking. Other, broader social efforts (i.e., those not limited to political or security elites), be they economic, environmental, educational, or health related, can help identify arenas for discreet cooperation during conflict as well as build public support for the negotiating process when more formal channels have dried up. Given the increasing political fragmentation in Israeli and Palestinian society and across the region (discussed above), not to mention the divisive impact of both new and old media, popular society-to-society initiatives assume greater importance. "The only way peace will happen," a civil society leader told the study group, "is if there's both top-down and bottom-up peace." U.S. negotiators and policy professionals, including those who direct our economic assistance programs, should pay closer attention to the bottom-up sector.

Foreign Aid and Economic Incentives

With few exceptions, such as the post-Wye assistance and free trade with and economic aid for Jordan, the net impact of our economic assistance too often has been to subsidize the status quo.

U.S. and international assistance to the PA seems to have accomplished little in the way of building Palestinian institutional and governance capability. "Governance," said a senior Palestinian official, reflecting on the Oslo years, too often was sacrificed for "expediency…. The thinking was that money and economics could sustain the process, [but] this was a huge mistake." Assistance to Palestinian security services in particular seems to have had no impact on the capability or willingness of the PA to stop terrorism. The mammoth international aid effort during the Oslo years, rather than improving living conditions for Palestinian society and building a constituency to support peace, instead propped up a bloated Palestinian bureaucracy and filled the gaps created by Israeli closures and severe economic downturns. "We failed … to make the advantages of peace palpable to enough of the Palestinians so that there was enough of a constituency for peace when push came to shove later," said a senior figure from the Clinton administration.

International assistance to Palestinians more than doubled in the years after the collapse of Oslo, due to both humanitarian concerns and the interest of donors in preserving the PA as a future negotiating partner. But the effect of this increase seemed negligible. One-time disbursements, such as the $20 million promised during Abu Mazen's 2005 visit to Washington, had little effect on his standing. Other issues, such as prisoner releases, lifting travel restrictions, and settlement expansion, all of which Abu Mazen had identified as being of great importance, did not receive as much U.S. attention, even though progress in these areas would have done much more to bolster the post-Arafat leadership.

In contrast, U.S. economic assistance to Jordan, which grew steadily in the years after the Israel-Jordan peace treaty, has played an important facilitation role. Following a model established with Egypt in the late 1970s, peace has been anchored in strategic ties between Israel, its neighbors, and Washington. As economic assistance and trade incentives with Jordan reach record levels and aid to Egypt remains high, future administrations must ensure that these inducements not only sustain Arab-Israeli peace but also support the reform and development agenda that remains vital for long-term stability in the region.

Summitry

International conferences have long been a feature of the Arab-Israeli diplomatic landscape as an effective tool for jump-starting negotiations and leveraging the combined influence of other outside parties. The United States has traditionally viewed conferences not as the goal of the peace process, but as a means to bring the parties together with outside support and thereby inject momentum for serious negotiations. The 1991 Madrid conference was a major diplomatic achievement because all sides were represented, including key international and regional players; it also launched a process of bilateral and multilateral negotiations. The Madrid agenda was broad, yet through consultations it was also refined to appeal to all sides. That said, the hard work of diplomacy will take place in more discreet settings, rather than in formal conference surroundings.

Still, summitry more recently has been misused. Rather than calling a summit in the context of a negotiation reasonably well prepared for at lower levels, recent administrations called for high-stakes meetings before the parties were ready to reach agreements.

The March 2000 Geneva summit, as detailed in earlier sections, was ill-conceived. Moreover, the study group was reminded that Arafat did not want to go to Camp David and argued for further negotiations on the secret track at Stockholm. Some on the U.S. side had reservations as well. The result was that Arafat was pressed to attend a meeting for which even the United States was unprepared. A U.S. draft agreement was shared first with the Israelis, then shown to Arafat with changes that reflected Israeli input, then abruptly withdrawn. In inviting the parties, Clinton also promised that no one would be blamed if the meeting failed. But promising no blame may have encouraged at least one of the parties—Arafat—to believe that there was no need to negotiate seriously. The blame card is a key element of U.S. influence in the peace process and should not be withdrawn preemptively unless major concessions are offered. Moreover, having made the promise, Clinton and senior administration figures then proceeded to heap blame on Arafat and the Palestinians, which likely undermined further diplomacy.

Bush 43 convened the Sharm el-Sheikh and Aqaba summits in 2003 to launch the Roadmap. National Security Adviser Rice was dispatched to the region, and a U.S. official—John Wolf— was appointed to monitor Roadmap performance. At the summit, the president promised to "ride herd" over the parties, leaving the impression that he and his administration would stay closely engaged. But both Israel and the Palestinians demonstrated immediately that they would not fulfill their commitments as stipulated under the Roadmap, and the United States did not respond. Thus, a summit wisely convened to launch a diplomatic initiative ended up in failure because there was no follow-up. The parties have run out of patience, said a former Bush 43 envoy, "for summits and meetings and the Tabas and Sharm el-Sheikhs. . . . I don't think these are very helpful unless there's a process that sets it up."

In the second half of 2007, President Bush and Secretary of State Rice sought to hold another peace conference. Initially, it was unclear whether Syria and other actors at odds with Washington would be represented, or whether the agenda would deal with the core issues or instead be weighted too much toward Palestinian institution building. It is always questionable whether U.S. diplomacy should have a major international meeting as a goal in and of itself. Such meetings should be used to help the parties narrow the boundaries of negotiations or to generate broad support for an initiative that is already under way; they should emerge from diplomatic activity or launch diplomatic activity so as to stimulate subsequent contacts and negotiations between the parties, as was the case with Madrid.

After months of diplomatic maneuvering, in which U.S. goals appeared to swing wildly from an ambitious attempt to frame permanent status negotiations to the more modest goal of renewing formal talks, Bush and Rice were able to bring Israeli and Palestinian leaders together in late November. The summit, held in Annapolis, Maryland, eventually elicited broad participation and support from across the Arab world, including Syria. The meeting came at a time when the United States sought greater Arab support in Iraq and in confronting Iran. Despite the modest success of Annapolis, the Bush 43 administration continued to signal that it would not go beyond a facilitation role, and that Israelis and Palestinians were expected to reach key understandings on their own.[8]

Assurances and Understandings

In conjunction with the convening of the Madrid conference, the Bush 41 administration offered the parties letters of assurances regarding U.S. policy.[9] Each letter was negotiated carefully, but the parties also understood that, first, the letters would not be secret from one other; second, the United States did not intend to use the letters to change existing policy; and third, the letters would not contradict or supersede the agreed-upon terms of reference for the conference. In contrast, Bush 43 offered Sharon a written U.S. commitment on settlement blocs and refugees in the context of helping Sharon overcome domestic Israeli opposition to disengagement—and, in effect, created new U.S. policy.

8. For the text of the "Joint Understanding" issued at Annapolis, see Appendix.

9. See the book's Web page at www.usip.org for examples of such letters.

Rather than using U.S. assurances to both help Israel and improve the prospects for peacemaking, the Bush 43 commitment contributed to a net deterioration in Israeli-Palestinian ties. "In terms of U.S. positions on final status issues," a senior U.S. official told the study group, it was not necessary "to pay as big a price as we did." Moreover, the official added, "It wasn't the neatest bureaucratic or most carefully thought through process in the world."

Assurances to one party have a way of becoming preconditions for diplomatic engagement with another. This was the case with commitments Kissinger made to Israel during peace negotiations in the mid-1970s: Over time, they became the basis for Washington's no-contact policy with the Palestine Liberation Organization (PLO). Although such conditions are important and necessary diplomatic tools, it is critical that they are used as a bridge, not a barrier, to peacemaking.

In January 2006, given Hamas's track record supporting terorism and rejecting past agreements, there was no way the United States could have engaged directly in diplomatic dealings following the group's victory in the Palestinian legislative elections. Moreover, as a donor, the United States had every right to condition its assistance. But in setting rigid, all-or-nothing preconditions for engagement after the election, U.S. diplomacy was perceived as confusing the positions of Hamas as a movement with the actions of the elected Palestinian government. The preconditions adopted by the Quartet closed off diplomacy.[10]

---

10. See the book's Web page at www.usip.org for the full text of the January 30, 2006, statement. The Quartet demanded that "all members of a future Palestinian government must be committed to nonviolence, recognition of Israel, and acceptance of previous agreements and obligations, including the Roadmap," adding that "it was inevitable that future assistance to any new government would be reviewed by donors against that government's commitment to the principles of nonviolence, recognition of Israel, and acceptance of previous agreements and obligations, including the Roadmap."

More adept, nuanced diplomacy would have reserved some flexibility for Washington and allowed the United States and its allies more space to test the Palestinian Authority's adherence to earlier comittments under Oslo. The Bush 43 administration was far more successful when it engaged in coercive diplomacy, as with Libya and North Korea, than when it refused to engage entirely.

The Bush 43 administration used a similar though less rigid no-contact approach with Syria beginning in early 2005. But here, too, the policy failed to achieve its goals and lead to significant changes in Syrian behavior in Iraq or Lebanon, or toward Iran or the Palestinians. Too often, the administration effectively ceded the diplomatic landscape to other actors with their own agendas. Both Syria and Saudi Arabia attempted to broker a Palestinian unity government without coordination from Washington. Iran responded to U.S. policy by deepening its ties to Syria and Hamas, earning Tehran new influence in the Arab-Israeli sphere.

In sum, these various instruments of statecraft, especially when employed repeatedly, should be used with strategic objectives in mind, not merely as instruments to buy time or give the appearance of progress. The cost may be a loss of credibility and degradation of an important diplomatic tool.

RECOMMENDATIONS FOR
FUTURE ADMINISTRATIONS

The next president will be dealing with an even more complex and involved situation in the Middle East than the one that Bush 43 inherited from Clinton. Current events suggest that this problematic international milieu will continue for several years until the United States can extricate itself from Iraq in a manner that does not result in even greater regional upheaval. Local conditions could rapidly deteriorate, particularly in Lebanon and the Palestinian territories. The president must confront the urgency of the U.S. troop presence in Iraq and Afghanistan, a looming confrontation with Iran, issues of energy security, and the uncertain world of international terrorism and the proliferation of weapons of mass destruction. Rebuilding alliances and shoring up the resolve of the international community to continue the struggle against terrorism will surely be among the president's highest priorities. In this respect, those voices calling for higher priority to the Arab-Israeli peace process could be drowned out in the swirl of policy debates and personnel choices that confront the next and future administrations. But this environment need not deter the next president from devoting energy and time to the Arab-Israeli peace process; indeed, it may well be the right context to press for action on that front.

The Arab-Israeli arena is a critical element of the strategic environment, and successful diplomacy there can create opportunities for the United States elsewhere in the region. If the president fails early on to establish the Middle East peace process as a priority, sooner or later the conflict will flare up and further complicate U.S. objectives. Waiting for the perfect moment for diplomacy is not an option. It will be up to the president to prioritize Arab-Israeli peacemaking, empower a foreign policy team that shares this view, and ensure that there is a senior focal point and a strong, experienced team within the administration to carry out its policy. At times, the president will need to be involved personally to convince Arabs and Israelis to take risks for peace.

Part of a renewed U.S. effort toward Arab-Israeli peace must be to restore the credibility and effectiveness of U.S. leadership, both in the peace process and in diplomacy more broadly. Despite its good intentions, strong domestic support, and intensive engagement, in its final, eleventh-hour attempts at Arab-Israeli peacemaking, the Clinton administration contributed to the collapse of the negotiations, bequeathing a mixed legacy to Bush 43. However, rather than chart a new, more productive, course, the Bush 43 administration effectively disengaged for close to eight years, acting as though White House pronouncements were sufficient to move the parties toward a settlement. Despite an attempt to jump-start Israeli-Palestinian negotiations late in the second term, the widely held perception was that the administration had abandoned the long-standing U.S. commitment to ending the conflict. Given this legacy, the next administration needs to develop a different model that combines presidential determination, leadership, and diplomatic follow-through to restore effectiveness to U.S. diplomacy in the Middle East.

Future administrations must avoid the temptation to substitute photo opportunities and ill-prepared conferences and summits for real diplomacy. Summits, conferences, and envoys have meaningful roles to play in a well-executed diplomatic game plan.

Well-timed meetings can galvanize parties to act, register progress made in quiet diplomacy, or impel new avenues of peacemaking. But such encounters need to be prepared for and part of a larger strategy. The summits of 2000 were not well prepared, even though there could have been value to meetings that defined progress to date and showed what still needed to be done. Bush 43 used the Aqaba summit in 2003 to launch the Roadmap, but his late 2007 meeting was less well prepared.

Likewise, the complex diplomatic environment should not persuade the next president to adopt a hands-off policy to the Arab-Israeli conflict. Even a casual study of the Bush 43 approach demonstrates that the absence of U.S. engagement does nothing to ameliorate problems in the region and could exacerbate them while driving allies away. Moreover, as the Bush 41 and Clinton administrations demonstrated, active U.S. mediation brings with it a variety of related benefits on other regional priorities, not to mention the contribution to bolstering key alliances in Europe and the region.

Among the most prominent challenges for the next president will be the strength of militant Islam and the determination of some to attack the United States and the West. The Arab-Israeli conflict has not been immune to it, and in some ways has incubated and stimulated it. The emergence of Hezbollah in the early 1980s, the rise to prominence of Hamas in the 1990s and its accession to power in Palestine in 2006, and the appearance of al Qaeda affiliates among Palestinians in Lebanon demonstrate that the festering Arab-Israeli conflict can fuel forces of ever-greater radicalism, and this factor alone will present future administrations with policy challenges unmatched by any predecessor.

The study group was not mandated to address the larger questions of militant Islam and whether regional stabilization must be a prelude to Arab-Israeli peace, but the track record of past decades suggests that heavy U.S. diplomatic engagement in the peace process supports both our relations with Arab states and the realization of our broader regional interests. Regional moderates have demonstrated that working toward Arab-Israeli peace addresses the challenge of dealing with militant Islamists. While there are surely a number of reasons for the Arab Summit's decisions in 2002 and 2007 to turn the policy of traditional Arab rejection of Israel on its head, surely one important aspect of this conceptual change related to the Arab world's realization that one of the strongest arguments against Islamist militancy would be a just and comprehensive Arab-Israeli peace settlement.

There is also reason for the president to establish conditions carefully for dialogue and engagement, as such conditions can unintentionally morph into barriers to communication. During the 1970s, 1980s, and 1990s, a core objective of the peace process was to bring increasing numbers of Arabs and Muslims into the orbit of peace; this must continue as an objective, and thus, the issue of who to boycott and what preconditions to attach to dialogue needs to be thought through wisely. Multilateral cooperation is particularly vital.

The next administration may need to deal with an additional issue, namely, the future of the two-state solution as an objective that attracts the support of Arabs and Israelis. Only in the last few years has the majority of both constituencies accepted the critical importance of there being two states in historic Palestine or Eretz Israel: the state of Israel and a state of Palestine, existing side by side in peace and mutual security. However, the failure of the Oslo process, the breakdown of the Palestinian and Syrian tracks, the Palestinian Intifada and Israel's tough counterterrorist response, the ongoing problems of Israeli settlements and occupation practices, the radicalization of Palestinian politics, continued acts of terrorism against Israelis, and increasing polarization across the region have all affected the psychology and political views of both Palestinians and Israelis.

It is impossible to know whether the two-state solution will remain viable for many more years. Every setback in peace diplomacy and every outbreak of violence has a negative effect on the attitudes supporting peace within Israeli and Arab societies. Despair, hostility, and mistrust have a way of hardening and giving rise to radical and destructive alternatives. The next president may not have much time to develop a way toward peace; if the administration fails early on to launch a serious diplomatic effort, the idea of a two-state solution will likely continue to erode.

Public opinion polls in Israel and the Palestinian territories continue to show majority support for a two-state solution that ends the conflict. It is a question, however, of whether support for two states—which requires concessions from both societies that cut to the core of their national credos and narratives—can be sustained in the onslaught of alternatives that opponents of the peace process offer. Ample historical evidence disproves the most pernicious of these ideas, but both the parties and the United States will need political courage and determination to maintain focus on achieving the compromises that would underpin the two-state solution.

For many decades, administrations articulated long-standing U.S. policy interests and could count on a strong bipartisan base of congressional and public support to pursue their national goals. The study group heard from our legislators that bipartisanship continues to be the watchword in the Arab-Israeli peace process, but only if there is strong presidential leadership focused on an agreed-upon goal of a reasonable, fair, and just peace that ensures security for all sides. There will be differences of view within the public, press, and Congress over tactics, but these differences can be contained so long as there is a durable and forward-looking strategy around which the president seeks to rally support.

Given the enormous challenges in organizing a new administration and setting up a national security decision-making process, a number of specific policy recommendations emerge from the study group's work.

First, the Arab-Israeli question ought to figure prominently in an early presidential speech, in which the White House need not articulate new policy, but simply send a loud and clear signal that the issue is high on the agenda. The administration might approach this speech with two tactical options: Either the president can deliver the speech and use it to suggest interest in early visits by Israeli and Arab leaders to discuss strategy, or the White House can invite regional leaders early on to visit Washington, using the initial consultations to shape the president's approach to the Arab-Israeli conflict.

Second, from the first day in office, the president ought to charge those responsible for the Middle East portfolio with developing a strategy that works to end the Arab-Israeli conflict. The study group heard a great deal about process and the danger that it can substitute for diplomacy. The right process is certainly important to bring conflicting parties together, but even a superb process will never substitute for purposeful diplomacy based on clear aims and objectives. What is achievable early on may necessarily fall short of a policy's ultimate ambition. But there should be no doubt—at home or in the region—that U.S. policy aims to achieve comprehensive and durable political settlements between Israel and its neighbors.

Third, U.S. diplomacy must prioritize locking in the gains of earlier negotiations, especially before public support in the region erodes or events on the ground further undermine prospects for a peaceful settlement. Washington needs to formalize and add permanence to U.S. positions on the core endgame issues of Jerusalem, refugees, security, and territory—in essence, putting forward a successor to the Clinton parameters. Then, the task would be to seek an international endorsement, preferably through the United Nations Security Council. Clearly defined parameters that capture the core trade-offs on the bilateral and multilateral tracks should be the centerpiece of U.S. policy. Given the stalemate between the parties and the urgent need to preserve negotiated outcomes, narrowing the confines of what is on the table is a fundamental task, essential to mobilize moderates and isolate rejectionists. Being clear and unambiguous about each of the core elements of the endgame not only provides long-term direction but guides the short-term choices Washington will have to make to preserve our preferred outcomes in the face of forces that pull away from a solution.

To move in such a direction, Washington will need to do its homework and prepare its own set of detailed proposals and bridging ideas on the core final-status issues. The next administration should quietly activate a back-office State Department operation to develop a menu of options and to plan U.S. positions. The Clinton administration, in its eleventh-hour attempt to strike a deal, was caught unprepared and then had to clumsily develop positions on complex issues such as Jerusalem at the very last minute. In 2007, the United States pushed for Israelis and Palestinians to return to final-status negotiations, but in choosing not to develop its own positions, the Bush 43 initiative was viewed as lacking substance. In the months leading up to the November 2007 Annapolis summit, when the parties could not agree on even the most general outlines of a negotiated settlement, U.S. diplomacy was hamstrung by our own accumulated failures in policy planning.

Fourth, Washington should invest in nontraditional diplomacy, including track II dialogue and people-to-people peacebuilding activities (described in Lesson 10, above). From the Bush 41 administration to the present, U.S. negotiators paid little attention to nontraditional diplomacy, which is partly reflected in the modest and episodic funding devoted to support such unofficial efforts. Nontraditional diplomacy is a low-cost, low-risk complement to the formal negotiating process, and given the distance between the parties and the turmoil of recent years, these activities—including private political and diplomatic contacts, military and security dialogues, youth and interreligious programming, and health, business, scientific, and cultural activities—have taken on even greater importance. However, nontraditional diplomacy also requires sustained investment and patience to see results; funders both in and out of government should take a long-term perspective, even as diplomats must understandably live in the moment.

Last, the next administration should keep an open mind about how to deploy the wide range of diplomatic instruments at its disposal. Tools that have not been employed wisely need to be assessed with a view to either invigorating them or finding alternative ways to proceed. The Quartet has been in existence for more than five years but has yet to prove its worth. Its future ought to be examined carefully to see whether it can become more effective. Similarly, some institutions created under the Oslo process may require alteration, such as the Ad Hoc Liaison Committee, a high-level body created to coordinate donor assistance to the Palestinians. Given the increasing need for third-party mechanisms on the ground, the committee may be a more effective policy tool if it expands its mandate and perhaps morphs into a regional contact group devoted to a wider set of issues, from monitoring security cooperation and facilitating access and movement to coordinating humanitarian and economic-development efforts. Washington needs to bolster its own diplomatic capacity on the ground, but it would make sense to do so in a way that leverages the assets of other outside actors.

A final note on Israel, Arabs, and U.S. policy: The study group heard a variety of perspectives on issues ranging from the role of Israel in trying to shape U.S. policy to the deference that some policymakers pay to Israeli domestic political concerns. Israel plays an outsized role in U.S. politics and diplomacy; it is a fact of life that transcends party politics and carries over from one administration to the next. The study group's Arab interlocutors recognized that part of what makes the U.S. role in the peace process so vital is the closeness of the U.S.-Israeli relationship. To the degree that Israel can rely on the constancy of U.S. support for its security and ultimate survival, it will be more willing to take risks for peace. What the next president needs to consider, therefore, is not the nature of our strategic relationship with Israel—this should be self-evident to anyone familiar with the history of the Middle East and politics and policy in Washington—but rather how to use the U.S.-Israeli relationship beneficially in the cause of peace. Most Arab actors seek a fair and effective U.S. approach, not one that diminishes the U.S.-Israeli relationship.

The converse is also true. The next president can be confident that the Middle East experts who work in the administration have strong knowledge about Israel and are sensitive to the special relations between our two countries, but the president also needs to ensure that the administration has expert and experienced diplomats familiar with Arab societies and able to understand the nuances and complexities of Arab domestic politics and the relationship between Arab politics and diplomacy. This should be self-evident, but it has not always proved to be the case over the past dozen or more years. One simple step is for an administration to assign value to reporting and analysis from our ambassadors and embassies, and to assign experienced career professionals to sensitive diplomatic positions.

The United States sees itself to this day as an honest broker in the Middle East, and U.S. diplomats honestly try to be fair in mediating between Arabs and Israelis. The next president will need to ensure that the manner in which we conduct our diplomacy results in the peoples of the region sharing this perception. Addressing asymmetries in the peace process—as this book has advocated—does not mean tilting away from Israel. Rather, it means restoring the U.S. role to its historical purpose of helping the parties achieve their core requirements. Restoring this role surely will require the ability to listen and learn, but also the political courage and the diplomatic wisdom to advance the United States' long-term commitment to the pursuit of peace in the Middle East.

TIMELINE

1967	
June	Six-Day War: Responding to signs of an imminent attack from neighboring Arab states, Israel launches preemptive strike, routs the Arab forces, and occupies Sinai, East Jerusalem, Gaza, the West Bank, and the Golan Heights. The fundamental calculus of the Arab-Israeli conflict shifts dramatically.
June 19	President Lyndon Johnson's Five Points speech becomes basis for UN Security Council Resolution (UNSCR) 242.
August–September	The "three nos" are announced at an Arab summit in Khartoum: no negotiation with Israel, no recognition of Israel, no peace with Israel.
November 22	UN Security Council Resolution 242 adopted. The resolution calls for "a just and lasting peace in the Middle East," based in part on "withdrawal of Israeli armed forces from territories occupied" in the Six-Day War. UN mediation launched under envoy Gunnar Jarring.

1968	
June–August 1970	War of Attrition: Israel and Egypt (with direct Soviet involvement) fight a grueling, low-level war across the Suez frontier.
1969	
December	After weeks of behind-the-scenes diplomacy, Secretary of State William Rogers publicly presents his peace plan, which focuses on Israel and Egypt and calls for demilitarized zones, free passage through the Suez Canal for all countries (including Israel), and a permanent peace settlement that sets the border along the "former international boundary between Egypt and the mandated territory of Palestine." The plan's rejection by Israel, Egypt, and the Soviet Union quickly ends the Nixon administration's first Arab-Israeli peace initiative.
1969–70	
	The Soviet Union dramatically steps up its involvement in the conflict and increases military aid to Egypt.
1970	
August 7	Israel and Egypt forge a cease-fire, with U.S. mediation; War of Attrition ends.

September	"Black September": Jordanian army drives out Palestine Liberation Organization (PLO) in bloody fighting. In response to Israel's cooperation in resolving the crisis, the Nixon administration throws more support to the Jewish state, approving large economic and military assistance packages and signaling a major shift in the U.S. approach.
September 28	Egyptian President Gamal Abdel Nasser dies, succeeded by his vice president, Anwar Sadat.
1971	
November 1	As the Arab-Israeli conflict is increasingly intertwined with Cold War U.S.-Soviet competition and Moscow upgrades its ties with Egypt and Syria, the United States steps up its support for Israel. In November the first U.S.-Israel memorandum of understanding (MOU) is reached, covering military aid and policy coordination.
1973	
October 6	Yom Kippur/October War: In a coordinated, surprise attack designed to break the diplomatic stalemate, Egypt and Syria go to war against Israel.
October 13	United States commences massive airlift to Israel.

October 19	President Nixon submits special $2.2 billion request to Congress for airlift to Israel.
October 22	UN Security Council Resolution 338 calls for an immediate cease-fire and reaffirms the terms of Resolution 242.
October 25	To forestall the threat of a major Soviet military intervention, U.S. forces go on worldwide alert, raising the specter of a direct superpower clash.
October 26	Cease-fire takes hold with troop withdrawals and armistice agreements yet to be settled.
Fall	Against the backdrop of the October War, Secretary of State Henry Kissinger plots a new approach for U.S. diplomacy: a step-by-step, U.S.-led framework for gradually moving toward a comprehensive Arab-Israeli settlement.
December	Attempting to create a diplomatic opening in the aftermath of the war, the United States organizes a peace conference in Geneva, cosponsored with Moscow.
1974	
January	Shuttle diplomacy by Kissinger leads to the first of two partial withdrawal and disengagement agreements signed by Israel and Egypt.

March	Nixon submits aid bill to Congress with unprecedented requests for Egypt and Jordan.
April	Nixon waives repayment of $1 billion in arms credits to Israel.
May 31	Following weeks of intensive U.S.-led diplomacy, Israel and Syria sign disengagement agreement; later in the year, a UN peacekeeping force is deployed to the Golan Heights. The following year, annual U.S. aid to Syria jumps from $0 to $100 million.
1975	
March	United States announces lifting of arms embargo on Egypt.
March 24	United States blames Israel for breakdown in talks with Egypt, announces "reassessment," freeze on new economic and military aid requests.
May 21	Seventy-six U.S. senators demand that President Gerald Ford be "responsive to Israel's economic and military needs."
Early June	Ford meets with Egyptian and Israeli leaders. Active U.S. mediation resumes; "reassessment" ends.

September 1	In a prelude to brokering a second Israeli-Egyptian disengagement agreement, Washington signs another MOU with Israel, pledging $2 billion in aid to Israel and committing to long-term supply of advanced weapons. The Ford administration also commits not to recognize or negotiate with the PLO until it recognizes Israel's right to exist and UNSCR 242 and 338.
September 4	Ford and Kissinger broker a second partial withdrawal and disengagement agreement signed by Israel and Egypt.
December	Intersectarian violence in Lebanon spirals into full-scale civil war. Syrian troops enter the fighting in June 1976, and remain in Lebanon until 2005.
1977	
January–November	President Jimmy Carter attempts to reconvene Geneva conference and return to the traditional U.S. approach of seeking a comprehensive settlement.
June 20	Menachem Begin elected prime minister of Israel.
November 19	Sadat begins a historic two-day visit to Jerusalem, becoming the first Arab leader to visit the Jewish state.

December 25–26	Sadat and Begin meet in Ismailiya, Egypt. Following Sadat's initiative and the Israeli-Egyptian diplomatic breakthrough, the Carter administration abandons its early ideas in favor of pushing for an Israeli-Egyptian peace treaty. Nevertheless, Carter resists leaving the Palestinian issue off the table, which he continues to view as key to the overall conflict.

1978

March	Israeli army launches Operation Litani and sends its military into southern Lebanon to combat PLO terrorists and other armed militant groups.
April 28	Carter asks Congress to approve triple arms package to Israel, Egypt, and Saudi Arabia.
June	Under U.S. and UN pressure, Israeli forces withdraw from Lebanon, retaining a "buffer zone" through a Lebanese proxy militia. United Nations Interim Force in Lebanon (UNIFIL) deployed.
July 18–19	Meeting at Leeds Castle, England, attended by Israeli, Egyptian, and U.S. delegations, produces early draft of the Camp David accords.

September 4–17	Camp David peace conference: With intensive U.S. involvement, led by President Carter, Sadat and Begin sign a framework Egyptian-Israeli peace agreement, as well as a second accord on behalf of the Palestinians that aims to establish Palestinian autonomy in the West Bank and Gaza. At Camp David, Washington promises to underwrite transfer of Israeli airbases from Sinai to Negev.
October–November	Negotiations for formal Israeli-Egyptian peace treaty held in Washington.
November 5	Arab countries vote against Camp David accords, offer Sadat $5 billion per year for ten years to abrogate agreement; Sadat declines the offer.
1979	
January 15	The shah of Iran flees.
March 7–13	Carter travels to Egypt and Israel to complete the negotiations over the peace treaty.
March 26	Begin and Sadat sign Israeli-Egyptian peace treaty in Washington. Israeli-Egyptian talks on Palestinian autonomy continue but never get off the ground.
1980	
July 30	Israeli parliament passes Jerusalem law, laying claim to an enlarged municipal area as Israel's "eternal, undivided capital."

1981	
July	U.S. mediator Philip Habib negotiates PLO-Israeli cease-fire agreement.
October 6	Sadat is assassinated in Egypt; Hosni Mubarak takes over as president, continues to implement peace treaty with Israel.
December 14	Israeli Knesset extends Israeli law to Golan Heights, effectively annexing the Syrian territory.
1982	
April	Israel completes military and civilian withdrawal from Sinai, in accordance with its peace treaty with Egypt.
June–August	Massive Israeli invasion of Lebanon, targeting PLO and Syrian forces, leads to an overall upsurge in the civil war, with Israeli army laying siege to Beirut. Yasser Arafat and PLO forces are evacuated with facilitation of U.S., French, and Italian forces.
September 1	President Ronald Reagan unveils new U.S. initiative (the Reagan Plan) to reach Arab-Israeli peace, based on Resolution 242 and the Camp David accords. Begin rejects it categorically.
September 16	Lebanese President Bashir Gemayel assassinated. Israeli forces occupy West Beirut.

September 16–18	Almost 2,000 Palestinian civilians in Sabra and Shatila are massacred by Lebanese Phalange militias, an event that sparks international outrage. Israeli Defense Minister Ariel Sharon later forced to resign over the killings, which took place in areas under Israeli military control.

1983

April 18	U.S. embassy in Beirut is destroyed in terrorist bombing.
May 17	Israel and Lebanon's Maronite government sign a U.S.-mediated peace treaty, which collapses the following year.
August	Begin resigns as Israeli prime minister; Yitzhak Shamir succeeds him.
October 23	U.S. Marine barracks in Beirut are destroyed in a massive suicide bombing; 241 U.S. servicemen are killed.

1984

February 21	Reagan orders U.S. forces to withdraw from Lebanon.
March 5	Acceding to Syrian pressure, Lebanon abrogates Lebanese-Israeli agreement.
September	Shimon Peres becomes prime minister of Israel as part of a rotation agreement with Likud's Yitzhak Shamir.

1985	
June	Israel withdraws most forces from Lebanon, retaining control over a twelve-mile-wide "buffer zone" on its northern border.
September	Peres launches Jordan-centered peace initiative, proposing an international conference, with U.S. encouragement. Shamir and Likud party oppose the idea of an international conference.
1986	
February	Jordan's King Hussein ceases effort to coordinate strategy with PLO chairman Yasir Arafat.
July	Peres meets with King Hassan II of Morocco.
September	Shamir replaces Peres as Israel's prime minister.
1987	
April	Peres, as foreign minister, meets Jordan's King Hussein privately in London and they agree on a landmark peace deal, but Shamir repudiates it. Peres asks Secretary of State George Shultz to adopt the plan as a U.S. initiative; Shultz declines.
December 9	First Intifada: Palestinian uprising begins in Gaza and spreads to West Bank, continues for several years.

1988	
February–April	Shultz attempts to revive peace process with shuttle mediation effort ("Shultz Plan"), but finds support lacking from several parties.
July	King Hussein cuts legal and administrative ties with the West Bank, effectively transferring control of the territory to the PLO and abandoning the idea of Jordan regaining some control of the West Bank.
December 13	Palestine National Council, the PLO's legislative body, renounces terrorism and accepts original UN partition plan (UN General Assembly Resolution 181), Israel's right to exist, and UN Security Council resolutions 242 and 338.
December 14	United States begins formal dialogue with the PLO in Tunis.
1989	
May	Shamir unveils peace proposal involving elections in the West Bank and Gaza; President George H.W. Bush and Secretary of State James Baker commence efforts to mediate revival of peace negotiations.
October	In Taif, Saudi Arabia, Lebanese members of parliament reach an accord to end the Lebanese civil war.
December	Syria reestablishes relations with Egypt, broken off after Camp David; Baker announces plan for Israeli-Palestinian negotiations.

1990	
March	Israeli coalition government collapses after Shamir rejects Baker plan.
June	After a terrorist attack on Israel, United States suspends its dialogue with the PLO.
July	Shamir forms new government, composed of Likud and several right-wing and religious parties.
August 2	Iraq invades Kuwait.
November	Bush meets with Syrian President Hafez al-Assad and assures him that the United States will convene an Arab-Israeli peace conference after Iraq is forced out of Kuwait. Syria agrees to join the U.S.-led coalition against Iraq.
1991	
January–February	Gulf War: Iraqi army forced out of Kuwait by U.S.-led coalition, including Saudi Arabia, Egypt, and Syria. During the war, Iraq attacks Israel with dozens of Scud missiles. Under U.S. pressure, Israel refrains from retaliating.
March 6	Bush addresses joint session of Congress, stressing U.S. commitment to resolve the Arab-Israeli conflict.
March–October	Baker makes eight shuttle-diplomacy trips to Middle East in attempt to arrange a regional peace conference between Arab states and Israel.

May	Israel announces plans to ask the United States for $10 billion in loan guarantees for immigrant absorption, which the Bush administration later links to a West Bank/Gaza settlement freeze; Baker gains Saudi participation in peace conference, as part of a Gulf Cooperation Council (GCC) observer delegation.
July 14	In a letter to Bush, Assad agrees to participate in the U.S.-sponsored regional peace conference, and to enter into direct talks with Israel.
August 1	Israeli Prime Minister Yitzhak Shamir agrees to attend regional peace conference.
September 6	Bush asks Congress for 120-day delay on Israeli request for loan guarantees.
October 30–November 1	The United States and USSR convene the Madrid peace conference. After Madrid, numerous rounds of bilateral and multilateral negotiations are held (Syria opts out of multilaterals).
1992	
January 28–29	Multilateral talks take place in Moscow, including Saudi participation. Later rounds take place in Lisbon, London, and multiple international venues.
February 24	Baker makes U.S. loan guarantees conditional on Israeli settlement freeze; relations remain tense between Shamir government and Bush administration.

March 17	White House rejects congressional compromise on loan guarantees to Israel.
Spring and Summer	Political campaigns in the United States and Israel slow negotiation process.
June 23	Likud defeated by Labor in Israeli elections; Yitzhak Rabin replaces Shamir as prime minister.
August 10–11	Bush, after meeting with Rabin in Maine, agrees to the $10 billion loan package, with a provision to deduct amounts equivalent to Israeli spending on settlements. Rabin does not formally agree to a freeze, but does signal strong commitment to the peace process.
October 5	Congress approves loan guarantees.
December	In response to the killing of several Israelis, Israel deports 415 Palestinian militants, mainly from Hamas, to southern Lebanon.
1993	
January 20	President William J. Clinton takes office; administration identifies Syria track as priority.
April 16	First Palestinian suicide bombing in Israel.
August 3	Rabin "deposit" to Secretary of State Warren Christopher on Syria peace deal.

Late August	Foreign Minister Shimon Peres briefs Christopher at Pt. Magu, CA, on the breakthrough at Oslo. Christopher turns down Peres's request that the United States claim sponsorship, instead agreeing to host the signing ceremony.
September 13	Israel-PLO Declaration of Principles (the Oslo Agreement) signed on White House lawn; Clinton presides over the historic Rabin-Arafat handshake; the heart of the agreement sets out a five-year interim period of Palestinian self-rule and Israeli withdrawals. Talks on a permanent settlement are set to begin midway through the interim period.
September 14	Israel and Jordan sign a Common Agenda in Washington.
October 1	Donor nations meet in Washington; $2.1 billion pledged to Palestinians.
December	First Oslo implementation deadline missed.
1994	
January 16	Clinton meets Assad in Geneva; Assad tells Clinton he is ready for "normal, peaceful" relations with Israel.
February 25	Baruch Goldstein, an Israeli settler, murders 29 Palestinians in Hebron; negotiations suspended.
May 4	Gaza-Jericho Agreement signed in Cairo; Palestinian self-rule begins.

May 10	Arafat calls for "jihad to liberate Jerusalem" in a speech at a Johannesburg mosque.
May 24	Israel and Syria announce terms of reference for U.S.-sponsored military talks.
July 1	Arafat arrives in Gaza from Tunis with cadre of PLO officials.
October 26	Israel and Jordan sign peace treaty at ceremony on the desert border between the two countries, in presence of Clinton.
October 27	Clinton meets Assad in Damascus in attempt to revive stalled Syrian-Israeli talks.
October 30	Casablanca summit on economic cooperation in the Middle East; leading figures attend from throughout the Arab world, Israel, Europe, and the United States. Regional economic summits are held annually until 1997.

1995

July 28	Legislation authorizing, but also restricting, aid to Palestinians advances in Congress; Peace Accord Monitoring Group set up in U.S. Senate. Middle East Peace Facilitation Act (MEPFA) renewed with tougher restrictions (Helms-Pell version): president must certify Palestinian compliance and report to Congress every six months.

September 28	After weeks of delay, Israeli-Palestinian Interim Agreement on the West Bank and Gaza signed in Washington (Oslo II); Palestinian self-rule set to expand from Gaza and Jericho to all major Palestinian cities and towns.
October 18–19	On heels of Oslo II, donor nations meet in Paris to renew aid program.
November	MEPFA lapses due to the State Department reorganization fight; Helms-Gilman block U.S. contribution to World Bank-sponsored Holst Fund, set up after Oslo to fund the Palestinian Authority's (PA) start-up costs.
November 4	Rabin assassinated; Peres takes over as prime minister.
December 27	First round of Israeli-Syrian talks at Wye Plantation.

1996

January 20	First PA elections; Arafat elected chairman/president, and Fatah wins control of 88-member Legislative Council; Hamas boycotts vote.
January 24	Second round of Israeli-Syrian talks at Wye Plantation.
February 28–March 3	Third round of Israeli-Syrian talks at Wye Plantation.
February 25–March 4	Three major suicide bombings in Israeli cities; Peres suspends Israeli-Syrian negotiations.

March 13	World leaders, including Clinton, gather for Summit of the Peacemakers in Sharm al-Sheikh, call for end to extremism and violence.
March 14	Clinton promises Israel $100 million in additional aid to fight terrorism.
April 11–26	Israel launches Operation Grapes of Wrath in southern Lebanon; U.S.-French mediation leads to Israel-Hezbollah cease-fire and international monitoring.
April 30	Clinton and Peres sign U.S.-Israeli counterterrorism accord. The Clinton administration is widely viewed as trying to bolster Peres in advance of the Israeli elections.
May 29	Benjamin Netanyahu of Likud elected prime minister, narrowly defeating Peres.
September 23–October 1	Armed clashes after Israel opens tunnel in Muslim Quarter in Jerusalem's Old City; 80 Palestinians and 15 Israeli soldiers killed.
October 2	Clinton extends duty-free trade to West Bank and Gaza.
1997	
January 17	Hebron agreement: last-ditch U.S.-Israeli-Palestinian talks achieve accord on implementing the Hebron provisions of the Interim Agreement, in particular Israeli troop redeployment. Christopher offers certain assurances in a Note for the Record.

June 17	Clinton announces Middle East Peace and Stability Fund, to provide resources to countries making a positive contribution to the peace process.
May	PA auditor Jarrar al-Qudwa announces that $326 million in Palestinian funds have been lost, due to mismanagement and corruption.
September	Israel suspends Oslo obligations following Palestinian suicide bombings in Jerusalem.
September 25	Mossad agents try to assassinate senior Hamas leader Khaled Mashal in Amman, but attack fails and Israeli agents arrested.
October 1	In response to demands from King Hussein of Jordan, Netanyahu orders the release of Sheikh Ahmed Yassin, Hamas founder, who returns to Gaza.
November	Secretary of State Madeleine Albright represents the United States at the fourth regional economic summit in Doha, Qatar, but most countries downgrade representation. Following Doha, the Casablanca process collapses, signaling a wider crisis for the multilateral track.

1998

| Winter–Spring | Oslo implementation languishes; increasing tension between Netanyahu government and Clinton administration over settlements and delays in Israeli West Bank redeployments. |

May	Netanyahu requests additional $1 billion in U.S. aid; American officials call the request "dead in the water," given Israeli delays in implementing the Interim Agreement.
June 30	According to the PA, $4.1 billion has been pledged since 1993 to the Palestinians, $2.4 billion disbursed.
July 27	U.S. bilateral assistance to Israel is restructured; $1.2 billion in annual economic aid will be phased out over ten years, reduced by $120 million each year, with half of the decrease going back to Israel in the form of military aid.
Summer–Fall	U.S. steps up mediation and offers its own proposal (13 percent) for the scope of the next Israeli West Bank redeployment.
October 23	After nine days at a Clinton-led summit in Maryland, Netanyahu and Arafat sign the Wye accord in Washington. Both sides agree to the U.S. 13 percent formula for West Bank withdrawals, as well as a host of new security and anti-incitement provisions. U.S. promises an additional $400 million to the Palestinians, and $1.2 billion to Israel for IDF redeployment. New aid also pledged to Egypt and Jordan.

November 30	Having delayed any new aid pledges as an incentive for progress between the parties, the United States convenes second donor conference in Washington to develop a five-year plan for international assistance to Palestinians.
December 14	Clinton—the first U.S. president to visit Gaza—addresses the Palestinian National Council, which votes to remove language from its charter calling for the destruction of Israel. During the visit to Israel and the Palestinian territories, the administration signals that Israel is not fulfilling its obligations under Wye.

1999

February 7	King Hussein dies.
March 4	United States informs Israel it will not receive Wye aid because it has not continued to implement the agreement.
May 4	End of Oslo accords' five-year transition period; Arafat raises possibility of a unilateral declaration of Palestinian statehood, but delays such a move.
May 17	Labor's Ehud Barak defeats Netanyahu, pledges to rejuvenate the peace process.
July 7	Barak takes office as Israeli prime minister.
July 17	During a White House visit, Barak promises Clinton a comprehensive peace deal in fifteen months. Clinton offers strong support to Barak.

September	Albright presides at signing ceremony for Sharm al-Sheikh Memorandum; Barak succeeds in renegotiating terms of 1998 Wye accord. Palestinian leaders sign on, but are angry at United States and Israel for re-opening Wye.
September	Clinton vetoes foreign aid bill; Republcan-controlled Congress underfunds Clinton's request for economic assistance for the peace process.
November	Congress approves compromise foreign aid bill, including supplemental funding for Israel, the Palestinians, Egypt, and Jordan, in accordance with the Wye agreement.
December 15–16	Syrian-Israeli talks resume in Washington after break of almost four years.

2000

January 3–10	Clinton presides at Syrian-Israeli talks at Shepherdstown, West Virginia; draft peace treaty discussed, but summit ends without agreement.
January 17	Third round of Syrian-Israeli talks postponed indefinitely.
March 21	Much-delayed Palestinian-Israeli final status negotiations at Bolling Air Force Base.
March 26	Clinton-Assad summit in Geneva; talks collapse within minutes, effectively shutting down Israeli-Syrian track.
May 4	Secret Israeli-Palestinian talks begin in Stockholm.

May 24	Israel unilaterally withdraws from southern Lebanon.
June	The UN Security Council certifies that Israel withdrew from Lebanon earlier in the year in accordance with UNSCR 425, despite claims later made by Hezbollah that the Israeli withdrawal was not complete.
June 10	Assad dies; his son, Bashar al-Assad, assumes the Syrian presidency.
July 11–25	Camp David II; Clinton and Barak publicly blame Arafat for failure of summit.
July 31–September 28	Series of secret meetings between negotiators Sa'eb Erekat and Gilad Sher.
September 28	Likud leader Ariel Sharon visits Temple Mount in Jerusalem; Palestinians launch Al-Aqsa Intifada.
October 16	Clinton attends Sharm al-Sheikh summit in an effort to stop violence and rescue the peace process.
October 22	Arab League suspends all regional economic cooperation with Israel.
November 21	Egypt recalls ambassador from Tel Aviv; Jordan withholds sending new ambassador to Israel.
December 10	Barak submits resignation.
Late December	Clinton presents U.S. "parameters" on core issues to Israel and Palestinian negotiating teams.

2001	
January 7	Central Intelligence Agency Director George Tenet brokers Cairo Understanding on security and movement.
January 18–28	Taba negotiations between PLO officials and Israeli officials; talks go beyond progress achieved at Camp David II, but break off as Israeli elections near.
January 20	Clinton leaves office; President George W. Bush inaugurated.
February 6	Sharon elected prime minister.
February 9	Bush administration disavows Clinton-era peace proposals.
April 30	Mitchell Committee/Sharm al-Sheikh fact-finding commission issues recommendations, including calls to end terrorism, renew security cooperation, and freeze Israeli settlement.
June 13	Tenet cease-fire plan accepted by Israelis and Palestinians, but not implemented.
July 19	Group of Eight (G-8) calls for implementation of Mitchell recommendations.
August 27	Israel assassinates Abu Ali Mustafa, leader of Popular Front for the Liberation of Palestine (PFLP).

August 25	Saudi Crown Prince Abdullah sends lengthy letter to Bush threatening to reconsider Saudi-U.S. ties and excoriating the administration over its handling of escalating Israeli-Palestinian violence.
August 29	Bush writes letter to Abdullah assuring support for a Palestinian state.
September 11	Terrorist attacks on World Trade Center and Pentagon.
September	In the aftermath of the attacks, Assad offers support to Bush in the war on terrorism; Syria cooperates in sharing intelligence on al Qaeda operatives in Europe, and reportedly turns over intelligence on suspects held in Syria.
September 26	Peres and Arafat agree on cease-fire and to restart joint security actions.
September 28	U.S.-Jordan Free Trade Agreement ratified and signed into law.
September	Quartet (United States, European Union, Russia, and United Nations) holds first informal meeting.
October 17	PFLP assassinates Rehavam Ze'evi, Israeli minister of tourism.
November 10	At UN General Assembly, Bush calls for a Palestinian state as laid out in Security Council resolutions.
November 19	Secretary of State Colin Powell gives speech at University of Louisville calling for two states.

November 19	General Anthony Zinni appointed U.S. envoy.
December 2	Bomb attacks kill 26 Israeli civilians in Jerusalem and Haifa.
December 3	Arafat's headquarters in Ramallah attacked by Israeli helicopters.
2002	
January 3	Israel seizes the *Karine A*, a PA-owned ship loaded with arms; Arafat denies knowledge of the arms shipment.
February 17	Public release of Crown Prince Abdullah's peace initiative.
March 12	UN Security Council Resolution 1397 endorses creation of a Palestinian state.
March 27	Hamas bombing in Netanya kills 30 Israelis, capping a month of terrorism in which many Israelis are killed. Zinni security work plan accepted by Israel but not Palestinians.
March 28	Arab League in Beirut adopts Crown Prince Abdullah's peace plan.
March 29	Israeli army launches Operation Defensive Shield, reoccupying major Palestinian cities in West Bank and besieging Arafat's headquarters in Ramallah.
April 14	Powell meets Arafat in Ramallah.
April 18	Powell returns to Washington without agreement to end violence and return to negotiations.

May 2	End of siege on Arafat's headquarters following U.S.-UN mediation.
June 23	PA launches 100 Days Reform Plan for governance.
June 24	In major speech, Bush calls for end of terrorism, "new" Palestinian leadership, and support for Palestinian statehood.
July 7	Basic Law for the Palestinian National Authority adopted; intended to be a provisional constitution until the establishment of a Palestinian state.
July 10	Quartet forms Task Force on Palestinian Reform.
September 17	Quartet presents preliminary Roadmap to peace.
2003	
March 7	Under pressure from Western donors to share power, Arafat creates position of PA prime minister and appoints Mahmoud Abbas.
March 20	U.S.-led war against Iraq begins.
April 14	Israel offers fourteen reservations on Roadmap; Sharon concedes the need for "painful concessions" on territory but refuses right of return for Palestinians.
April 16	Congress appropriates $9 billion in loan guarantees for Israel to use within 1967 borders over three years.

April 30	Quartet officially announces Roadmap peace plan; Abbas accepts without reservations.
May 2	Powell visits Damascus for talks with Assad, outlines conditions for continued positive relations between the United States and Syria, including closure of terrorist group offices, such as Hamas; Powell announces that Syria has agreed to close some offices, but Syrian press contradicts these assurances.
May 25	Sharon's cabinet accepts "steps defined" in Roadmap with reservations.
June	John Wolf appointed to set up Roadmap Monitoring Mission.
June 3–4	Bush, Abbas, and Sharon meet in Aqaba; Abbas pledges to use peaceful means to attain Palestinian goals and Sharon agrees to remove unauthorized "outposts" and to support Palestinian state with "territorial contiguity."
July 8	Bush approves $20 million in direct aid to PA for infrastructure projects.
August 6	Israel releases 339 Palestinian prisoners.
August 19	Roadmap process derailed after Palestinian suicide bombing of Jerusalem bus kills 21 Israelis; Israeli forces target Hamas leaders in response.

September 2	UN Security Council Resolution 1559 calls for withdrawal of all foreign forces from Lebanon.
September 6	Abbas resigns as PM, citing lack of support from Arafat, the United States, and Israel.
September 7	Palestinian Legislative Council (PLC) speaker Ahmed Qureia (Abu Ala) appointed as prime minister.
September 9	Palestinian groups' cease-fire ends with attacks in Jerusalem and Tzrifin.
October	The Geneva Accord, a Swiss government-funded track II project, offers a detailed draft Israeli-Palestinian peace treaty.
October 5	Israel bombs terrorist camp in Syria, in response to a suicide bombing.
November 26	United States deducts $289.5 million of $3 billion in loan guarantees to Israel because of separation wall and settlement construction beyond the 1967 border.
December 1	Assad, in a *New York Times* interview, says Syria is willing to resume negotiations with Israel without preconditions.
December 12	Bush signs the Syria Accountability and Lebanese Sovereignty Restoration Act (SALSA) into law; the Act calls for sanctions on Syria to discourage its support of terrorism, its occupation of Lebanon, and its interference in Iraq.
December 18	Sharon announces unilateral Gaza disengagement plan at Herzliya Conference.

2004	
February 13	White House says unilateral withdrawal from Gaza could reduce tension but affirms that final settlement must be negotiated.
March 22	Israeli military assassinates Hamas leader Sheikh Ahmed Yassin.
April 14	Bush-Sharon exchange of letters; Bush offers support for Sharon disengagement plan, declares that Israel should be able to keep existing "population centers" in the West Bank and that Palestinian refugees should be resettled in Palestine, not Israel.
April 19	Dov Weissglas, Sharon's chief of staff, provides written commitment to Secretary of State Condoleezza Rice on dismantlement of "illegal settlement outposts," and a range of other commitments on settlements.
June 6	Israeli government approves Sharon's disengagement plan.
July 9	International Court of Justice issues opinion against Israel's separation barrier, calling for construction to cease immediately.
October 6	In *Ha'aretz* interview Weissglas says disengagement provides the "formaldehyde" to freeze any political process with Palestinians.
November 11	Arafat dies in Paris; Abbas takes over as PLO chairman and Rawhi Fattouh becomes interim PA president.

December 8	Bush authorizes $20 million in direct aid to the PA to pay Israeli utility companies.
2005	
January 9	Mahmoud Abbas elected PA president.
February 7	General William Ward appointed U.S. Middle East security coordinator.
February 8	Sharon, Abbas, Mubarak, and King Abdullah II meet in Sharm el-Sheikh; Sharon and Abbas agree to end violence and military operations and Israel agrees to withdraw from Palestinian cities.
February 14	Former Lebanese Prime Minister Rafiq al-Hariri assassinated in Beirut; Syria becomes the focus of renewed international pressure as calls are made for a UN tribunal.
February 19	Jordan restores its ambassador to Israel, marking the first time since August 2000 that the position has been occupied.
March 1	In a London speech, Secretary of State Condoleezza Rice calls for "free and fair" Palestinian parliamentary elections, urging a "more representative Palestinian Authority."
March 10	Sasson report documents high-level Israeli government support for settlements and settlement "outposts," traces wide-ranging pattern of illegality.
March 12	Hamas announces intention to participate in PLC elections.

March 17	Egyptian ambassador to Israel restored to his post.
March 19	Palestinian organizations sign Cairo Declaration, committing to a unilateral period of calm (tahdi'a) through 2005 and the holding of legislative and local elections without delay.
April 15	Quartet appoints James Wolfensohn as special envoy for Gaza disengagement.
April 26	Syria completes withdrawal of its military from Lebanon.
May 26	Abbas travels to Washington; Bush asserts that "changes to 1949 armistice lines must be mutually agreed to."
End of May	Bush approves $50 million direct transfer to the PA in attempt to bolster Abbas.
June 3	Abbas delays parliamentary election, citing ongoing dispute over election laws.
July	G-8 leaders pledge $3 billion to Palestinians at Gleneagles summit in United Kingdom.
July 5	Hamas announces it will resume firing Qassam rockets into Israel following unilateral Israeli withdrawal from Gaza.
August 17–23	Israel unilaterally withdraws from all Gaza settlements and four small West Bank settlements.

August 29	Sharon announces no further unilateral or coordinated disengagements; all future steps will fall under the rubric of the Roadmap.
September 25	Hamas announces cessation of armed Gaza operations.
October 20	First UN report on the Hariri assassination points to high-level Syrian involvement; members of the Security Council discuss sanctions against Syria, though no action is taken.
October 26	Israel and Egypt agree to open key Gaza-Egypt border crossings.
November 15	Rice brokers Agreement on Movement and Access (AMA), intended to assure regular flow of people and goods in and out of Gaza; agreement falls apart within weeks. General Keith Dayton replaces Ward as U.S. Middle East security coordinator.
November 25	Rafah border crossing reopens under EU monitoring, but remains closed for long stretches in 2006 and 2007.
December	Hamas fares well in municipal elections in West Bank and Gaza.
December 28	Quartet declares that any future PA cabinet must respect Israel's right to exist in peace, and end violence and terrorism.
2006	
January 4	Sharon suffers stroke; Ehud Olmert becomes acting prime minister.

January 25	Hamas wins PLC elections; Olmert refuses to negotiate until Hamas disarms, revokes its call for the destruction of Israel, and accepts all prior Israel-PLO agreements.
January 30	Quartet announces it will weigh future aid against PA's commitment to nonviolence, recognition of Israel, and acceptance of previous agreements and obligations.
February 16	Sense of Congress resolutions pass urging Bush administration to cut PA aid unless Hamas recognizes Israel; Rice assures Senate that no aid will go to Hamas government.
February 27	European Union announces $140 million aid package to PA caretaker government.
March 29	Hamas government is installed.
March 30	Quartet criticizes Hamas-led PA for not adhering to January 30 conditions, institutes wide-ranging aid boycott.
March	Bush withholds delivery of $45 million (of previously approved $50 million) in direct funds to the PA.
April 14	Olmert elected prime minister; pledges to set Israel's final borders, and commits to establish a security border unilaterally if agreement with Palestinians cannot be reached.
April 30	With Hamas in power, economic paralysis in Gaza, and the Quartet largely on the sidelines, Wolfensohn steps down as special envoy.

June 25	After abduction of Israeli soldier Gilad Shalit, Israel closes the Rafah border crossing.
July 12	Israel-Hezbollah War begins with cross-border Hezbollah raid; two Israeli soldiers are abducted and two others killed. More than 1,300 Lebanese and 150 Israelis are killed in the conflict; 250,000 flee from northern Israel, and 350,000 evacuate southern Lebanon.
August 14	Cease-fire takes effect, ending Israel-Hezbollah War.
September 1	European Union announces a Temporary International Mechanism (TIM) to provide direct social, medical, and energy assistance to the Palestinians.
September	Fighting erupts between Fatah and Hamas forces in the West Bank.
October 20	Fatah and Hamas agree to a cease-fire.
December	The bipartisan Iraq Study Group recommends a major diplomatic initiative for Iraq, including direct U.S. engagement with Syria and Iran; the group also calls for greater U.S. efforts to revive the Arab-Israeli peace process, arguing it is vital to a larger regional strategy to stabilize Iraq.
December 28	Israeli officials confirm shipment via Egypt of direct military aid to Abbas's Fatah security forces, through Kerem Shalom crossing.

2007	
January 20	Talks in Damascus between Hamas leader Khaled Mashal and Abbas fail to result in agreement on a Palestinian unity government.
February 8	In Mecca, Saudi Arabia brokers a power-sharing agreement between Hamas and Fatah. The United States opposes the move, and reiterates that compliance with the Quartet's three conditions—recognition of Israel, acceptance of previous agreements, and renouncing violence—remains the prerequisite for resuming international aid to the PA.
March 27	Bush asks Congress to approve $59 million in direct aid to Fatah security forces.
June	In renewed factional fighting, Hamas military forces seize total control of Gaza, routing the U.S.-trained and Fatah-allied Palestinian security forces. President Abbas denounces the move as a Hamas "coup" and sets up an emergency government in Ramallah, headed by former finance minister Salam Fayyad.
Summer	Israel seals Gaza from the outside world, allowing in only minimal humanitarian assistance. Links between Gaza and the West Bank, divided between Hamas and Fatah political authority, are effectively severed.

June 18	United States lifts aid embargo on Palestinian government, joining the European Union and others in bolstering Abbas and Fayyad, and promising up to $86 million in aid. Rice announces an additional $40 million U.S. contribution to the United Nations Relief and Works Agency (UNRWA) to assist Palestinians in Gaza.
June 27	Former British prime minister Tony Blair named Quartet special envoy to the Middle East.
July 16	Bush calls for a meeting of Israel, the Palestinians, and neighboring Arab states, to be chaired by Rice; the meeting is to be held in late 2007, with the goal of moving "forward on a successful path to a Palestinian state."
Late November	Bush, Olmert, and Abbas meet at Annapolis conference, issue "Joint Understanding," and agree to immediately resume final status negotiations. There is a large Arab presence at the meeting, including Syria. United States pledges to "monitor and judge" each party's obligations under the Roadmap.

SELECTED DOCUMENTS AND PRIMARY SOURCES

This appendix includes a number of official documents, peace initiatives, formal agreements, draft accords, and official correspondence, with a focus on the U.S. role in the Arab-Israeli peace process since the end of the Cold War:

- Letter of Invitation to Madrid Peace Conference (1991)
- Declaration of Principles on Interim Self-Government Arrangements (The "Oslo Accord")
- The Wye River Memorandum (October 1998)
- Draft Israel-Syria Peace Treaty (Prepared by the United States at the Shepherdstown Talks, January 2000)
- U.S. Draft of a Framework Israeli-Palestinian Peace Treaty (Presented to the Parties During the Camp David II Summit, July 13, 2000)
- Clinton Parameters
- Bush Rose Garden Speech (June 2002)
- The Quartet's "Roadmap" Peace Plan (April 2003)
- Sharon-Bush Exchange of Letters (April 2004)
- Letter from Dov Weissglas to Condoleezza Rice (April 2004)
- Israeli-Palestinian "Joint Understanding" (Presented by President Bush at the Annapolis Conference, November 27, 2007)

Letter of Invitation to Madrid Peace Conference (1991)[1]

After extensive consultations with Arab states, Israel and the Palestinians, the United States and the Soviet Union believe that an historic opportunity exists to advance the prospects for genuine peace throughout the region. The United States and the Soviet Union are prepared to assist the parties to achieve a just, lasting and comprehensive peace settlement, through direct negotiations along two tracks, between Israel and the Arab states, and between Israel and the Palestinians, based on United Nations Security Council Resolutions 242 and 338. The objective of this process is real peace.

Toward that end, the president of the U.S. and the president of the USSR invite you to a peace conference, which their countries will co-sponsor, followed immediately by direct negotiations. The conference will be convened in Madrid on October 30, 1991.

President Bush and President Gorbachev request your acceptance of this invitation no later than 6 P.M. Washington time, October 23, 1991, in order to ensure proper organization and preparation of the conference.

Direct bilateral negotiations will begin four days after the opening of the conference. Those parties who wish to attend multilateral negotiations will convene two weeks after the opening of the conference to organize those negotiations. The co-sponsors believe that those negotiations should focus on region-wide issues of water, refugee issues, environment, economic development, and other subjects of mutual interest.

The co-sponsors will chair the conference which will be held at ministerial level. Governments to be invited include Israel, Syria, Lebanon and Jordan. Palestinians will be invited and attend as part of a joint Jordanian-Palestinian delegation. Egypt will be invited to the conference as a participant. The European Community will be a participant in the conference, alongside the United States and the Soviet Union and will be represented by its presidency. The Gulf Cooperation Council will be invited to send its secretary-general to the conference as an observer, and GCC member states will be invited to participate in organizing the negotiations on multilateral issues. The United Nations will be invited to send an observer, representing the secretary-general.

1. U.S. Embassy in Israel. "Letter of Invitation to Madrid Peace Conference." October 31, 2000. http://telaviv.usembassy.gov/publish/peace/madrid.htm (accessed on October 1, 2007).

The conference will have no power to impose solutions on the parties or veto agreements reached by them. It will have no authority to make decisions for the parties and no ability to vote on issues of results. The conference can reconvene only with the consent of all the parties.

With respect to negotiations between Israel and Palestinians who are part of the joint Jordanian-Palestinian delegation, negotiations will be conducted in phases, beginning with talks on interim self-government arrangements. These talks will be conducted with the objective of reaching agreement within one year. Once agreed, the interim self-government arrangements will last for a period of five years; beginning the third year of the period of interim self-government arrangements, negotiations will take place on permanent status. These permanent status negotiations, and the negotiations between Israel and the Arab states, will take place on the basis of Resolutions 242 and 338.

It is understood that the co-sponsors are committed to making this process succeed. It is their intention to convene the conference and negotiations with those parties who agree to attend.

The co-sponsors believe that this process offers the promise of ending decades of confrontation and conflict and the hope of a lasting peace. Thus, the co-sponsors hope that the parties will approach these negotiations in a spirit of good will and mutual respect. In this way, the peace process can begin to break down the mutual suspicions and mistrust that perpetuate the conflict and allow the parties to begin to resolve their differences. Indeed, only through such a process can real peace and reconciliation among the Arab states, Israel and the Palestinians be achieved. And only through this process can the peoples of the Middle East attain the peace and security they richly deserve.

Declaration of Principles on Interim Self-Government Arrangements (the "Oslo Accord")[2]

Signed on the White House Lawn, September 13, 1993

2. Although the Declaration of Principles was not an American document, it was embraced by the United States and came to define an era of peacemaking; the text of the subsequent accord, the September 1995 "Interim Agreement" (Oslo II) is available on this book's Web page at www.usip.org. United Nations, "Declaration of Principles on Interim Self-Government Arrangements," UN Security Council General Assembly, 48th session, 48th year, agenda item 10, www.un.org (accessed on October 1, 2007).

The Government of the State of Israel and the PLO team (in the Jordanian-Palestinian delegation to the Middle East Peace Conference) (the "Palestinian Delegation"), representing the Palestinian people, agree that it is time to put an end to decades of confrontation and conflict, recognize their mutual legitimate and political rights, and strive to live in peaceful coexistence and mutual dignity and security and achieve a just, lasting and comprehensive peace settlement and historic reconciliation through the agreed political process. Accordingly, the two sides agree to the following principles:

Article I: AIM OF THE NEGOTIATIONS

The aim of the Israeli-Palestinian negotiations within the current Middle East peace process is, among other things, to establish a Palestinian Interim Self-Government Authority, the elected Council (the "Council"), for the Palestinian people in the West Bank and the Gaza Strip, for a transitional period not exceeding five years, leading to a permanent settlement based on Security Council resolutions 242 (1967) and 338 (1973). It is understood that the interim arrangements are an integral part of the whole peace process and that the negotiations on the permanent status will lead to the implementation of Security Council resolutions 242 (1967) and 338 (1973).

Article II: FRAMEWORK FOR THE INTERIM PERIOD

The agreed framework for the interim period is set forth in this Declaration of Principles.

Article III: ELECTIONS

1. In order that the Palestinian people in the West Bank and Gaza Strip may govern themselves according to democratic principles, direct, free and general political elections will be held for the Council under agreed supervision and international observation, while the Palestinian police will ensure public order.

2. An agreement will be concluded on the exact mode and conditions of the elections in accordance with the protocol attached as Annex I, with the goal of holding the elections not later than nine months after the entry into force of this Declaration of Principles.

3. These elections will constitute a significant interim preparatory step toward the realization of the legitimate rights of the Palestinian people and their just requirements.

Article IV: JURISDICTION

Jurisdiction of the Council will cover West Bank and Gaza Strip territory, except for issues that will be negotiated in the permanent status negotiations. The two sides view the West Bank and the Gaza Strip as a single territorial unit, whose integrity will be preserved during the interim period.

Article V: TRANSITIONAL PERIOD AND PERMANENT STATUS NEGOTIATIONS

1. The five-year transitional period will begin upon the withdrawal from the Gaza Strip and Jericho area.

2. Permanent status negotiations will commence as soon as possible, but not later than the beginning of the third year of the interim period, between the Government of Israel and the Palestinian people's representatives.

3. It is understood that these negotiations shall cover remaining issues, including: Jerusalem, refugees, settlements, security arrangements, borders, relations and cooperation with other neighbours, and other issues of common interest.

4. The two parties agree that the outcome of the permanent status negotiations should not be prejudiced or preempted by agreements reached for the interim period.

Article VI: PREPARATORY TRANSFER OF POWERS AND RESPONSIBILITIES

1. Upon the entry into force of this Declaration of Principles and the withdrawal from the Gaza Strip and the Jericho area, a transfer of authority from the Israeli military government and its Civil Administration to the authorized Palestinians for this task, as detailed herein, will commence. This transfer of authority will be of a preparatory nature until the inauguration of the Council.

2. Immediately after the entry into force of this Declaration of Principles and the withdrawal from the Gaza Strip and Jericho area, with the view to pro-

moting economic development in the West Bank and Gaza Strip, authority will be transferred to the Palestinians in the following spheres: education and culture, health, social welfare, direct taxation and tourism. The Palestinian side will commence in building the Palestinian police force, as agreed upon. Pending the inauguration of the Council, the two parties may negotiate the transfer of additional powers and responsibilities, as agreed upon.

Article VII: INTERIM AGREEMENT

1. The Israeli and Palestinian delegations will negotiate an agreement on the interim period (the "Interim Agreement").

2. The Interim Agreement shall specify, among other things, the structure of the Council, the number of its members, and the transfer of powers and responsibilities from the Israeli military government and its Civil Administration to the Council. The Interim Agreement shall also specify the Council's executive authority, legislative authority in accordance with Article IX below, and the independent Palestinian judicial organs.

3. The Interim Agreement shall include arrangements, to be implemented upon the inauguration of the Council, for the assumption by the Council of all of the powers and responsibilities transferred previously in accordance with Article VI above.

4. In order to enable the Council to promote economic growth, upon its inauguration, the Council will establish, among other things, a Palestinian Electricity Authority, a Gaza Sea Port Authority, a Palestinian Development Bank, a Palestinian Export Promotion Board, a Palestinian Environmental Authority, a Palestinian Land Authority and a Palestinian Water Administration Authority and any other Authorities agreed upon, in accordance with the Interim Agreement, that will specify their powers and responsibilities.

5. After the inauguration of the Council, the Civil Administration will be dissolved, and the Israeli military government will be withdrawn.

Article VIII: PUBLIC ORDER AND SECURITY

In order to guarantee public order and internal security for the Palestinians of the West Bank and the Gaza Strip, the Council will establish a strong police force, while Israel will continue to carry the responsibility for defending against external threats, as well as the responsibility for overall security of Israelis for the purpose of safeguarding their internal security and public order.

Article IX: LAWS AND MILITARY ORDERS

1. The Council will be empowered to legislate, in accordance with the Interim Agreement, within all authorities transferred to it.
2. Both parties will review jointly laws and military orders presently in force in remaining spheres.

Article X: JOINT ISRAELI-PALESTINIAN LIAISON COMMITTEE

In order to provide for a smooth implementation of this Declaration of Principles and any subsequent agreements pertaining to the interim period, upon the entry into force of this Declaration of Principles, a Joint Israeli-Palestinian Liaison Committee will be established in order to deal with issues requiring coordination, other issues of common interest and disputes.

Article XI: ISRAELI-PALESTINIAN COOPERATION IN ECONOMIC FIELDS

Recognizing the mutual benefit of cooperation in promoting the development of the West Bank, the Gaza Strip and Israel, upon the entry into force of this Declaration of Principles, an Israeli-Palestinian Economic Cooperation Committee will be established in order to develop and implement in a cooperative manner the programmes identified in the protocols attached as Annex III and Annex IV.

Article XII: LIAISON AND COOPERATION WITH JORDAN AND EGYPT

The two parties will invite the Governments of Jordan and Egypt to participate in establishing further liaison and cooperation arrangements between the Government of Israel and the Palestinian representatives, on the one hand, and the Governments of Jordan and Egypt, on the other hand, to promote cooperation between them. These arrangements will include the constitution of a Continuing Committee that will decide by agreement on the modalities of admission of persons displaced from the West Bank and Gaza Strip in 1967, together with necessary measures to prevent disruption and disorder. Other matters of common concern will be dealt with by this Committee.

Article XIII: REDEPLOYMENT OF ISRAELI FORCES

1. After the entry into force of this Declaration of Principles, and not later than the eve of elections for the Council, a redeployment of Israeli military forces in the West Bank and the Gaza Strip will take place, in addition to withdrawal of Israeli forces carried out in accordance with Article XIV.

2. In redeploying its military forces, Israel will be guided by the principle that its military forces should be redeployed outside populated areas.

3. Further redeployments to specified locations will be gradually implemented commensurate with the assumption of responsibility for public order and internal security by the Palestinian police force pursuant to Article VIII above.

Article XIV: ISRAELI WITHDRAWAL FROM THE GAZA STRIP AND JERICHO AREA

Israel will withdraw from the Gaza Strip and Jericho area, as detailed in the protocol attached as Annex II.

Article XV: RESOLUTION OF DISPUTES

1. Disputes arising out of the application or interpretation of this Declaration of Principles, or any subsequent agreements pertaining to the interim period, shall be resolved by negotiations through the Joint Liaison Committee to be established pursuant to Article X above.

2. Disputes which cannot be settled by negotiations may be resolved by a mechanism of conciliation to be agreed upon by the parties.

3. The parties may agree to submit to arbitration disputes relating to the interim period, which cannot be settled through conciliation. To this end, upon the agreement of both parties, the parties will establish an Arbitration Committee.

Article XVI: ISRAELI-PALESTINIAN COOPERATION CONCERNING REGIONAL PROGRAMMES

Both parties view the multilateral working groups as an appropriate instrument for promoting a "Marshall Plan", the regional programmes and other programmes, including special programmes for the West Bank and Gaza Strip, as indicated in the protocol attached as Annex IV.

Article XVII: MISCELLANEOUS PROVISIONS

1. This Declaration of Principles will enter into force one month after its signing.

2. All protocols annexed to this Declaration of Principles and Agreed Minutes pertaining thereto shall be regarded as an integral part hereof.

   DONE at Washington, D.C., this thirteenth day of September 1993.

   For the Government of Israel:

   (Signed) Shimon PERES

   For the PLO:

   (Signed) Mahmoud ABBAS

   Witnessed by:

   The United States of America

   (Signed) Warren CHRISTOPHER

   The Russian Federation

   (Signed) Andrei V. KOZYREV

[*For Annex I, II, III, IV and the "Agreed Minutes," see the book's Web page at www.usip.org.*]

The Wye River Memorandum (October 1998)[3]

The following are steps to facilitate implementation of the Interim Agreement on the West Bank and Gaza Strip of September 28, 1995 (the "Interim Agreement") and other related agreements including the Note for the Record of January 17, 1997 (hereinafter referred to as "the prior agreements") so that the Israeli and Palestinian sides can more effectively carry out their reciprocal responsibilities, including those relating to further redeployments and security respectively. These steps are to be carried out in a parallel phased approach in accordance with this Memorandum and the attached time line. They are subject to the relevant terms and conditions of the prior agreements and do not supersede their other requirements.

---

3. U.S. Department of State. "The Wye River Memorandum." Permanent electronic archive of White House Office documents. http://www.state.gov/www/regions/nea/981023_interim_agmt.html (accessed October 3, 2007).

I. Further Redeployments

A. Phase One and Two Further Redeployments

1. Pursuant to the Interim Agreement and subsequent agreements, the Israeli side's implementation of the first and second F.R.D. will consist of the transfer to the Palestinian side of 13% from Area C as follows:

1% to Area (A) 12% to Area (B)

The Palestinian side has informed that it will allocate an area/areas amounting to 3% from the above Area (B) to be designated as Green Areas and/or Nature Reserves. The Palestinian side has further informed that they will act according to the established scientific standards, and that therefore there will be no changes in the status of these areas, without prejudice to the rights of the existing inhabitants in these areas including Bedouins; while these standards do not allow new construction in these areas, existing roads and buildings may be maintained.

The Israeli side will retain in these Green Areas/Nature Reserves the overriding security responsibility for the purpose of protecting Israelis and confronting the threat of terrorism. Activities and movements of the Palestinian Police forces may be carried out after coordination and confirmation; the Israeli side will respond to such requests expeditiously.

2. As part of the foregoing implementation of the first and second F.R.D., 14.2% from Area (B) will become Area (A).

B. Third Phase of Further Redeployments

With regard to the terms of the Interim Agreement and of Secretary Christopher's letters to the two sides of January 17, 1997 relating to the further redeployment process, there will be a committee to address this question. The United States will be briefed regularly.

II. Security

In the provisions on security arrangements of the Interim Agreement, the Palestinian side agreed to take all measures necessary in order to prevent acts of terrorism, crime and hostilities directed against the Israeli side, against individuals falling under the Israeli side's authority and against their property, just as the Israeli side agreed to take all measures necessary in order to prevent acts of terrorism, crime and hostilities directed against the Palestinian side, against individuals falling under the Palestinian side's authority and against their property. The two sides also agreed to take legal measures against offenders within their jurisdiction and to prevent incitement against each other by any organizations, groups or individuals within their jurisdiction.

Both sides recognize that it is in their vital interests to combat terrorism and fight violence in accordance with Annex I of the Interim Agreement and the Note for the Record. They also recognize that the struggle against terror and violence must be comprehensive in that it deals with terrorists, the terror support structure, and the environment conducive to the support of terror. It must be continuous and constant over a long-term, in that there can be no pauses in the work against terrorists and their structure. It must be cooperative in that no effort can be fully effective without Israeli-Palestinian cooperation and the continuous exchange of information, concepts, and actions.

Pursuant to the prior agreements, the Palestinian side's implementation of its responsibilities for security, security cooperation, and other issues will be as detailed below during the time periods specified in the attached time line:

A. Security Actions

1. Outlawing and Combating Terrorist Organizations

(a) The Palestinian side will make known its policy of zero tolerance for terror and violence against both sides.

(b) A work plan developed by the Palestinian side will be shared with the U.S. and thereafter implementation will begin immediately to ensure the systematic and effective combat of terrorist organizations and their infrastructure.

(c) In addition to the bilateral Israeli-Palestinian security cooperation, a U.S.-Palestinian committee will meet biweekly to review the steps being taken to eliminate terrorists calls and the support structure that plans, finances, supplies and abets terror. In these meetings, the Palestinian side will inform the U.S. fully of the actions it has taken to outlaw all organizations (or wings of organizations, as appropriate) of a military, terrorist or violent character and their support structure and to prevent them from operating in area under its jurisdiction.

(d) The Palestinian side will apprehend the specific individuals suspected of perpetrating acts of violence and terror for the purpose of further investigation, and prosecution and punishment of all persons involved in acts of violence and terror.

(e) A U.S.-Palestinian committee will meet to review and evaluate information pertinent to the decisions on prosecution, punishment or other legal measures which affect the status of individuals suspected of abetting or perpetrating acts of violence and terror.

2. Prohibiting Illegal Weapons

(a) The Palestinian side will ensure an effective legal framework is in place to criminalize, in conformity with the prior agreements, any importation, manufacturing or unlicensed sale, acquisition or possession of firearms, ammunition or weapons in areas under Palestinian jurisdiction.

(b) In addition, the Palestinian side will establish and vigorously and continuously implement a systematic program for the collection and appropriate handling of all such illegal items it accordance with the prior agreements. The U.S. has agreed to assist in carrying out this program.

(c) A U.S.-Palestinian-Israeli committee will be established to assist and enhance cooperation in preventing the smuggling or other unauthorized introduction of weapons or explosive materials into areas under Palestinian jurisdiction.

3. Prevention Incitement

(a) Drawing on relevant international practice and pursuant to Article XXII (1) of the Interim Agreement and the Note for the Record, the Palestinian side will issue a decree prohibiting all forms of incitement to violence or terror, and establishing mechanisms for acting systematically against all expressions or threats of violence or terror. This decree will be comparable to the existing Israeli legislation which deals with the same subject.

(b) A U.S.-Palestinian-Israeli committee will meet on a regular basis to monitor cases of possible incitement to violence or terror and to make recommendations and reports on how to prevent such incitement. The Israeli, Palestinian and U.S. sides will each appoint a media, specialist, a law enforcement representative, an educational specialist and a current or former elected official to the committee.

B. Security Cooperation

The two sides agree that their security cooperation will be based on a spirit of partnership and will include, among other things, the following steps:

1. Bilateral Cooperation

There will be full bilateral security cooperation between the two sides which will be continuous, intensive and comprehensive.

2. Forensic Cooperation

There will be an exchange of forensic expertise, training, and other assistance.

3. Trilateral Committee

In addition to the bilateral Israeli-Palestinian security cooperation, a high-ranking U.S.-Palestinian-Israeli committee will meet as required and not less than biweekly to assess current threats, deal with any impediments to effective security cooperation and coordination and address the steps being taken to combat terror and terrorist organizations. The committee will also serve as a forum to address the issue of external support for terror. In these meetings, the Palestinian side will fully inform the members of the committee of the results of its investigations concerning terrorist suspects already in custody and the participants will exchange additional relevant information. The committee will report regularly to the leaders of the two sides on the status of cooperation, the results of the meetings and its recommendations.

C. Other Issues

(a) The Palestinian side will provide a list of its policemen to the Israeli side in conformity with the prior agreements.

(b) Should the Palestinian side request technical assistance, the U.S. has indicated its willingness to help meet those needs in cooperation with other donors.

(c) The Monitoring and Steering Committee will, as part of its functions, monitor the implementation of this provision and brief the U.S.

2. PLO Charter

The Executive Committee of the Palestine Liberation Organization and the Palestinian Central Council will reaffirm the letter of 22 January 1998 from PLO Chairman Yasir Arafat to President Clinton concerning the nullification of the Palestinian National Charter provisions that are inconsistent with the letters exchanged between the PLO and the Government of Israel on 9-10 September 1993. PLO Chairman Arafat, the Speaker of the Palestine National Council, and the Speaker of the Palestinian Council will invite the members of the PNC, as well as the members of the Central Council, the Council, and the Palestinian Heads of Ministries to a meeting to be addressed by President Clinton to reaffirm their support for the peace process and the aforementioned decisions of the Executive Committee and the Central Council.

3. Legal Assistance in Criminal Matters

Among other forms of legal assistance in criminal matters, the requests for arrest and transfer of suspects and defendants pursuant to Article II (7) of Annex IV of the Interim Agreement will be submitted (or resubmitted) through the mechanism of the Joint Israeli-Palestinian Legal Committee and will be responded to in conformity with Article II (7) (f) of Annex IV of the Interim Agreement within the 12 week period. Requests submitted after the eighth week will be responded to in conformity with Article II (7) (f) within four weeks of their submission. The United States has been requested by the sides to report on a regular basis on the stops being taken to respond to the above requests.

4. Human Rights and the Rule of Law

Pursuant to Article XI (1) of Annex I of the Interim Agreement, and without derogating from the above, the Palestinian Police will exercise powers and responsibilities to implement this Memorandum with due regard to internationally accepted norms of human rights and the rule of law, and will be guided by the need to protect the public, respect human dignity, and avoid harassment.

III. Interim Committees And Economic Issues

1. The Israeli and Palestinian sides reaffirm their commitment to enhancing their relationship and agree on the need actively to promote economic development in the West Bank and Gaza. In this regard, the parties agree to continue or to reactivate all standing committees established by the Interim Agreement, including the Monitoring and Steering Committee, the Joint Economic Committee (JEC), the Civil Affairs Committee (CAC), the Legal Committee, and the Standing Cooperation Committee.

2. The Israeli and Palestinian sides have agreed on arrangements which will permit the timely opening of the Gaza Industrial Estate. They also have concluded a "Protocol Regarding the Establishment and Operation of the International Airport in the Gaza Strip During the Interim Period."

3. Both sides will renew negotiations on Safe Passage immediately. As regards the southern route, the sides will make best efforts to conclude the agreement within a week of the entry into force of this Memorandum. Operation

of the southern route will start as soon as possible thereafter. As regards the northern route, negotiations will continue with the goal of reaching agreement as soon as possible. Implementation will take place expeditiously thereafter.

4. The Israeli and Palestinian sides acknowledge the great importance of the Port of Gaza for the development of the Palestinian economy, and the expansion of Palestinian trade. They commit themselves to proceeding without delay to conclude an agreement to allow the construction and operation of the port in accordance with the prior agreements. The Israeli-Palestinian Committee will reactivate its work immediately with a goal of concluding the protocol within 60 days, which will allow commencement of the construction of the port.

5. The two sides recognize that unresolved legal issues adversely affect the relationship between the two peoples. They therefore will accelerate efforts through the Legal Committee to address outstanding legal issues and to implement solutions to these issues in the shortest possible period. The Palestinian side will provide to the Israeli side copies of all of its laws in effect.

6. The Israeli and Palestinian sides also will launch a strategic economic dialogue to enhance their economic relationship. They will establish within the framework of the JEC an Ad Hoc Committee for this purpose. The committee will review the following four issues: (1) Israeli purchase taxes; (2) cooperation in combating vehicle theft; (3) dealing with unpaid Palestinian debts; and (4) the impact of Israeli standards as barriers to trade and the expansion of the A1 and A2 lists. The committee will submit an interim report within three weeks of the entry into force of this Memorandum, and within six weeks will submit its conclusions and recommendations to be implemented.

7. The two sides agree on the importance of continued international donor assistance to facilitate implementation by both sides of agreements reached. They also recognize the need for enhanced donor support for economic development in the West Bank and Gaza. They agree to jointly approach the donor community to organize a Ministerial Conference before the end of 1998 to seek pledges for enhanced levels of assistance.

IV. Permanent Status Negotiations

The two sides will immediately resume permanent status negotiations on an accelerated basis and will make a determined effort to achieve the mutual goal of reaching an agreement by May 4, 1999. The negotiations will be continuous and without interruption. The United States has expressed its willingness to facilitate these negotiations.

V. Unilateral Actions

Recognizing the necessity to create a positive environment for the negotiations, neither side shall initiate or take any step that will change the status of the West Bank and the Gaza Strip in accordance with the Interim Agreement.

ATTACHMENT: Time Line

This Memorandum will enter into force ten days from the date of signature.
Done at Washington, DC this 23rd day of October 1998.
For the Government of the State of Israel: Benjamin Netanyahu
For the PLO: Yassir Arafat
Witnessed by: William J. Clinton, The United States of America

[For the Timeline annex, please see this book's Web page at www.usip.org.]

Draft Israel-Syria Peace Treaty (Prepared by the United States at the Shepherdstown Talks, January 2000)[4]

PREAMBLE

The Government of the State of Israel and the Government of the Syrian Arab Republic:

Aiming at the achievement of a just, lasting and comprehensive peace in the Middle East based on Security Council resolutions 242 and 338 and within the framework of the peace process initiated at Madrid on 31 October 1991;

Reaffirming their faith in the purposes and principles of the Charter of the

---

4. *Ha'aretz.* "A Framework for Peace Between Israel and Syria: The Draft Peace Treaty Presented by the Clinton Administration to Jerusalem and Damascus." January 15, 2000. Accessed via Lexis-Nexis at www.lexis.com (accessed October 3, 2007).

United Nations and recognizing their right and obligation to live in peace with each other, as well as with all states, within secure and recognized boundaries;

Desiring to establish mutual respect and to develop honorable, friendly and good neighborly relations;

Resolved to establish permanent peace between them in accordance with this Treaty.

Have agreed as follows:

Article I: ESTABLISHMENT OF PEACE AND SECURITY WITHIN RECOGNIZED BOUNDARIES

1. The state of war between Israel and Syria (hereinafter "the Parties") is hereby terminated and peace is established between them. The Parties will maintain normal, peaceful relations as set out in Article III below.

2. The permanent secure and recognized international boundary between Israel and Syria is the boundary set forth in Article II below. The location of the boundary has been commonly agreed (Syrian position: and is based on the June 4, 1967 line) (Israeli position: taking into account security and other vital interests of the Parties as well as legal considerations of both sides). Israel will (S: withdraw) (I: relocate) all its armed forces (S: and civilians) behind this boundary in accordance with Annex – of this Treaty. (S: Thereafter, each Party will exercise its full sovereignty on its side of the international boundary, including as agreed in this Treaty.)

3. To enhance the security of both Parties, agreed security measures will be implemented in accordance with Article IV below.

4. The time line at Annex – sets forth an agreed schedule for synchronized implementation of this and the other Articles of this Treaty.

Article II: INTERNATIONAL BOUNDARY

1. The international boundary between Israel and Syria is as shown on the mapping materials and co-ordinates specified in Annex –. This boundary is the permanent, secure and recognized international boundary between Israel and Syria and supercedes any previous boundary or line of demarcation between them.

2. The Parties will respect the inviolability of this boundary and of each other's territory, territorial waters and airspace.

3. A Joint Boundary Commission is hereby established. Its functions and activities are set out in Annex –.

Article III: NORMAL PEACEFUL RELATIONS

1. The Parties will apply between them the provisions of the Charter of the United Nations and the principles of international law governing relations among states in time of peace. In particular:

   a. they recognize and will respect each other's sovereignty, territorial integrity and political independence and right to live in peace within secure and recognized boundaries; and

   b. they will establish and develop friendly and good neighborly relations, will refrain from the threat or use of force, directly or indirectly, against each other, will cooperate in promoting peace, stability and development in their region and will settle all disputes between them by peaceful means.

2. The Parties will establish full diplomatic and consular relations, including the exchange of resident ambassadors.

3. The Parties recognize a mutuality of interest in honorable and good neighborly relations based on mutual respect and for this purpose will:

   a. promote beneficial bilateral economic and trade relations including by enabling the free and unimpeded flow of people, goods and services between the two countries.

   b. remove all discriminatory barriers to normal economic relations, terminate economic boycotts directed at the other Party, repeal all discriminatory legislation, and cooperate in terminating boycotts against either Party by third parties.

   c. promote relations between them in the sphere of transportation. In this regard, the Parties will open and maintain roads and international border crossings between the two countries, cooperate in the development of rail links, grant normal access to its ports for vessels and cargoes of the other or vessels or cargoes destined for or coming from that Party, and enter into normal civil aviation relations.

    d. establish normal postal, telephone, telex, data facsimile, wireless and cable communications and television relay services by cable, radio and satellite between them on a non-discriminatory basis in accordance with relevant international conventions and regulations; and

    e. promote cooperation in the field of tourism in order to facilitate and encourage mutual tourism and tourism from third countries.

       Annex–sets forth the agreed procedures for establishing and developing these relations, (I: including the schedule for the attainment of relevant agreements as well as arrangements concerning the Israelis and Israeli communities in areas from which Israeli forces will be relocated pursuant to Article I).

4. The Parties undertake to ensure mutual enjoyment by each other's citizens of due process of law within their respective legal systems and before their courts.

Notes (I) Components of normal peaceful relations which require further discussion: cultural relations; environment; interconnection of electricity grids; energy; health and medicine; and agriculture.

(II) Other possible areas for consideration: combating crime and drugs; anti-incitement cooperation; human rights; places of historical and religious significance and memorials; legal cooperation in the search for missing persons.

Article IV: SECURITY

A. Security Arrangements

Recognizing the importance of security for both Parties as an important element of permanent peace and stability, the Parties will employ the following security arrangements to build mutual confidence in the implementation of this Treaty and to provide for the security needs of both Parties:

1. Areas of limitation of forces and capabilities, including limitations on their readiness and activities, and on armaments, weapon system and military infrastructure, as described in Annex –.

2. Within the areas of limitation of forces and capabilities, the establishment of a demilitarized zone (I: encompassing both the area from which Israeli forces will be relocated and the existing Area of Separation established under

the Agreement on Disengagement between Israeli and Syrian Forces of 31 May 1974) (S: of equal scope on both sides of the border). As described in Annex –, no military forces, armaments, weapon systems, military capabilities, or military infrastructure will be introduced into the demilitarized zone by either Party and only a limited civil police presence may be deployed in the area. (I: Both sides agree not to fly over the demilitarized zone without special arrangements.)

3. Early warning capabilities, including an early warning ground station on Mt. Hermon (I: with an effective Israeli presence) (S: operated by the United States and France under their total auspices and responsibilities). Arrangements for the unimpeded, efficient and continuous operation of this station are as detailed in Annex –.

4. A monitoring, inspection and verification mechanism (I: composed of the two Parties and a multinational component and including on-site technical means) (S: through an international presence), to monitor and supervise the implementation of the security arrangements.

Details regarding these security arrangements, including their scope, positioning and nature, as well as other security arrangements, are specified in Annex –.

B. Other Security Measures

As further steps to ensure a permanent cessation of hostilities of any form between the Parties or from their territories against each other.

1. Each Party undertakes to refrain from cooperating with any third party in a hostile alliance of a military character and will ensure that territory under its control is not used by any military forces of a third party (including their equipment and armaments) in circumstances that would adversely affect the security of the other Party.

2. Each Party undertakes to refrain from organizing, instigating, inciting, assisting or participating in any acts or threats of violence against the other Party, its citizens or their property wherever located, and will take effective measures to ensure that no such acts occur from, or are supported by individuals on, its territory or territory under its control. In this regard, without prejudice to the basic rights of freedom of expression and association, each Party will take necessary and effective measures to prevent the entry, presence and operation in its territory of any group or organization, and their infrastructure, which threatens the security of the other Party by the use of, or incite-

ment to the use of, violent means.

3. Both Parties recognize that international terrorism in all its forms threatens the security of all nations and therefore share a common interest in the enhancement of international cooperative efforts to deal with this problem.

C. Cooperation and Liaison in Security Matters

The Parties will establish a direct liaison and coordination mechanism between them as described in Annex – to facilitate implementation of the security provisions in this Treaty. Its responsibilities will include: direct and real-time communication on security issues, minimization of friction along the international border, addressing any problems arising during the implementation process, helping to prevent errors or misinterpretations, and maintaining direct and continuous contacts with the monitoring, inspection and verification mechanism.

Article V: WATER

1. The Parties recognize that full resolution of all water issues between them constitutes a fundamental element in ensuring a stable and lasting peace. (S: Based on relevant international principles and practices), the Parties have agreed to establish (I: arrangements that will ensure the continuation of Israel's current use in quantity and quality of all) (S: mutually agreeable arrangements with respect to water quantities and quality from) the surface and underground waters in the areas from which Israeli forces will (I: relocate) (S: withdraw) pursuant to Article I, as detailed in Annex –. (I: The arrangements should include all necessary measures to prevent contamination, pollution or depletion of the Kinneret/Tiberias and Upper Jordan River and their sources.)

2. For the purposes of this Article and Annex –, the Parties will establish (I: a Joint Water Committee and a supervision and enforcement mechanism) (S: a Joint Administrative Board). The composition, mandate and mode of operations of the (I: Joint Water Committee and the supervision and enforcement mechanism) (S: Joint Administrative Board) will be as detailed in Annex –.

3. The Parties have agreed to cooperate on water-related matters, as detailed in Annex –, (I: including ensuring the quantity and quality of water allocated to Israel under other agreements concerning water originating in Syria.)

Article VI: RIGHTS AND OBLIGATIONS

1. This Treaty does not affect and shall not be interpreted as affecting in any way the rights and obligations of the Parties under the Charter of the United Nations.

2. The Parties undertake to fulfill in good faith their obligations under this Treaty, without regard to action or inaction of any other Party and independently of any instrument external to this Treaty.

3. The Parties will take all the necessary measures for the application in their relations of the provisions of the multilateral conventions to which they are Parties, including the submission of appropriate notification to the Secretary General of the United Nations and other depositories of such conventions. They will also abstain from actions that would curtail the rights of either Party to participate in international organizations to which they belong in accordance with the governing provisions of those organizations.

4. The Parties undertake not to enter into any obligation in conflict with this Treaty.

5. Subject to Article 103 of the United Nations Charter, in the event of a conflict between the obligations of the Parties under the present Treaty and any of their other obligations, the obligations under this Treaty will be binding and implemented.

Article VII: LEGISLATION

The Parties undertake to enact any legislation necessary in order to implement the Treaty, and to repeal any legislation that is inconsistent with the Treaty.

Article VIII: SETTLEMENT OF DISPUTES

Disputes between the Parties arising out of the interpretation or application of the present Treaty shall be settled by negotiation.

Article IX: FINAL CLAUSES

1. This treaty shall be ratified by both Parties in conformity with their respective constitutional procedures. It shall enter into force on the exchange of instru-

ments of ratification and shall supercede all previous bilateral agreements between the Parties.

2. The Annexes and other attachments attached to this Treaty shall constitute integral parts thereof.

3. The Treaty shall be communicated to the Secretary General of the United Nations for registration in accordance with the provisions of Article 102 of the Charter of the United Nations.

DONE THIS DAY ------ IN -------- IN THE ENGLISH, HEBREW AND ARABIC LANGUAGES, ALL LANGUAGES BEING EQUALLY AU-THENTIC. IN CASE OF ANY DIVERGENCE OF INTERPRETATION, THE ENGLISH TEXT WILL BE AUTHORITATIVE.

U.S. Draft of a Framework Israeli-Palestinian Peace Treaty (Presented to the Parties During the Camp David II Summit, July 13, 2000)[5]

7/13 (10pm)(2d FAPS)

{The purpose of this paper is to facilitate discussions between the parties on the core permanent status issues. It is in the form of a draft FAPS, but does not include all the issues the parties may wish to include in their FAPS nor does it address each issue with the degree of specificity that the parties may desire. The paper does not represent a U.S. position. The I: and P: language is only a US estimation based on discussion with the parties and is not intended to bind or prejudice the positions of the parties. The alternative possible solutions (ALT:) provided are intended to facilitate discussions and not to reflect the position of any of the parties.}

Israeli-Palestinian Framework Agreement on Permanent Status

Preamble

The Government of the State of Israel and the PLO, representing the Palestinian people ("the Parties");

5. Quandt, William B. *Peace Process: American Diplomacy and the Arab-Israeli Conflict Since 1967*, 3rd ed. Berkeley and Los Angeles: University of California Press, 2005. Online appendices, Web site of the Brookings Institution. http://www.brookings.edu/press/appendix/peaceprocessappen_aa.htm (accessed September 28, 2007).

REAFFIRMING their determination to put an end to the decades of confrontation and conflict and to live in peaceful coexistence, mutual dignity and security based on a just, lasting, and comprehensive peace settlement and historic reconciliation through the agreed political process;

RECOGNIZING each other's right and the right of its people for a peaceful and secure existence within secure and recognized boundaries free from threats or acts of force;

CONFIRMING that this Agreement (the "FAPS") is concluded within the framework of the Middle East peace process initiated in Madrid in October 1991 and pursuant to the Declaration of Principles and other agreements and letters between the Parties thereafter;

REITERATING their commitment to the United Nations Security Council Resolutions 242 and 338 and confirming their understanding that the FAPS is based upon and will lead to the implementation of Resolutions 242 and 338 between them;

VIEWING the FAPS as providing the basis for the resolution of the Israeli-Palestinian conflict and as an historical milestone in the creation of peace in the entire Middle East and between the entire Arab and Muslim worlds and Israel;

HEREBY AGREE AS FOLLOWS:

Article I: The Permanent Status Agreement and the End of the Israeli-Palestinian Conflict

1. The foregoing Preamble is an integral part of this Agreement.

2. This Agreement constitutes the framework for resolving all the issues reserved for permanent status negotiations. It sets forth principles, mechanisms and schedules for resolving each of these issues.

3. As necessary and mutually agreed, the provisions of the FAPS will be elaborated by the Parties in a comprehensive agreement on the permanent status issues [P: by September 13, 2000,] [I: by the date of the establishment of the Palestinian State] which together with the FAPS will constitute "the Permanent Status Agreement." However, any such further agreement or understanding will be consistent with and subordinate to the FAPS, which is intended to serve as the fundamental basis for resolving the permanent status issues and any related claims between the Parties;

4. [I: The conclusion of the FAPS marks the end of the conflict between the parties.] [P: The end of conflict between the parties will occur with the full implementation of the comprehensive agreement on permanent status.]

[ALT: The FAPS accordingly embodies the decision of the Parties to end their historic conflict.] The FAPS establishes their commitment not to raise any additional claims relating to the permanent status issues, either for themselves or on behalf of others.

5. [I: The end of conflict will lead to a final resolution of the prisoner issue through the release of prisoners by Israel.] [P: All Palestinian prisoners will be released by Israel upon the conclusion of the FAPS.]

6. The Parties agree that implementation of each provision of the FAPS, as elaborated upon in any subsequent agreement or understandings, shall constitute a complete, conclusive, and irrevocable resolution of the issues addressed by that provision.

Article 2: The State of Palestine and its Relations with the State of Israel

1. [P: The PLO confirms] [I: It is understood and agreed] that the exercise of the right of the Palestinian people to self-determination will take place through the establishment of a State of Palestine [P: one September 13, 2000] [I: by DMY] in the territories defined in this Agreement.

2. On the basis of the undertaking in this Agreement, Israel will support the establishment of the State of Palestine in the territories define in this Agreement.

3. The Israeli and Palestinian states will respect each other's sovereignty, territorial integrity and political and economic independence and will not seek to intervene in each other's internal affairs or represent the citizens of the other State. The Israeli and Palestinian states will conduct themselves in conformity with the UN Charter and the norms of international law.

4. Upon the establishment of the State of Palestine, Israel and the Palestinian State will confer formal recognition on each other and establish full diplomatic relations. In addition, the two states will call upon other countries to recognize the Palestinian State and, for those countries which have not already done so, to recognize the state of Israel, and to enter into normal relations with both states.

5. The State of Palestine will assume the responsibilities of the PLO and the Palestinian Authority under this Agreement and any other agreements between the Parties that are in force, as well as any agreements concluded by the PLO for the benefit of the Palestinian Authority.

6. The Israeli and Palestinian states will establish a relationship of peaceful coex-

istence. The two states will endeavor to enhance Israeli-Palestinian cooperation and coordination in all fields of common concern for their mutual benefit. This will include, among others, spheres of civil affairs, dialogue between their legislative bodies, comprehensive programs for law enforcement and legal assistance in criminal and civil matters, development of the common border regions between the two states, and promoting non-governmental civil society cooperation. The two states will also devote special attention to the development of joint programs in the areas of culture and education with the aim of promoting reconciliation between their respective peoples.

7. The Israeli and Palestinian states will create the appropriate atmosphere for a lasting peace by promulgating laws to put an end to incitement for terror and violence, by vigorously enforcing them and through the appropriate programs in their respective educational systems.

8. The Israeli and Palestinian States will work together to enhance regional cooperation and coordination.

Article III: Borders, Settlements and Territorial Arrangements

1. The permanent border between the State of Israel and the State of Palestine is set forth in the map attached to this Agreement. The delineation of the border is based upon and will lead to the implementation of the United Nations Security Council Resolutions 242 and 338. It is designed to provide the maximum territory for the Palestinian State while meeting vital Israeli needs.

2. In the area of the Gaza Strip the border will be the June 4, 1967 line.

3. In the area of the West Bank,

   a. The western border of the Palestinian state [I: will be delineated taking into account the 1967 lines, the realities on the ground and the strategic needs of Israel] [P: will be the June 4, 1967 line].

   ALT 1: The western border of the Palestinian State will be based on the 1967 lines with agreed modifications to reflect, inter alia, demographic realities and strategic concerns of the parties.

   [I: with modifications so that at least 80 percent of the settlers residing in blocs of settlements with reasonable contours will have continuity with and will be under Israeli sovereignty] [P: with any modifications compensated by territory of equal size and value].

   ALT 1: The percentage of the area to be incorporated by Israel to accom-

modate approximately 80% of the settlers would be minimal and therefore would not require reciprocal adjustments in territory.

ALT 2: A larger annexation by Israel to incorporate approximately 80% of
the settlers will require compensation for the territorial adjustment.

b. The eastern border of the Palestinian State will be [P: the boundary between Jordan and the West Bank] [I: adjacent to a strip of Israeli sovereign territory along the boundary between Jordan and the West Bank,
with links to Jordan]

ALT 1: A joint sovereignty arrangement.

ALT 2: Israeli sovereignty for a specified period of time.

ALT 3: Palestinian sovereignty but with a continuing Israeli military
presence along a narrow strip (Either for limited period of time or for
longer period.)

ALT 4: Palestinian sovereignty with limited adjustments in the border to
allow Israel to meet vital security needs.

ALT 5: Palestinian sovereignty that includes a 3rd party presence.

c. The remainder of the West Bank [P: will be under Palestinian sover-
eignty] [I: will include limited territories under Israeli control for security
purposes for an agreed period at the end of which they will be divided
between two states on an agreed ration of 7:1 (or 8:1) for the Palestinian
State].

ALT 1: The area that will become Palestinian under the 7:1 (or 8:1) ratio
will be specified in the agreement so that the total territory that will fall
under Palestinian sovereignty will be defined at the outset.

ALT 2: In the 7:1 (or 8:1) ratio, the area that constitutes the 1 part will
come under Palestinian sovereignty by a date certain as specified in the
agreement.

N.B. Leasing may be considered as a tool to resolve this issue.

4. Neither Israeli settlers nor Palestinians will be required to leave their communities as a result of the establishment of the final borders. Those who choose
to remain in areas in which they are not citizens [P: will be subject to local
law] [I: will be able to maintain their collective communal identity] in accordance with transitional arrangements set forth in the Transitional Arrangements Annex.

5. In the context of the comprehensive territorial arrangements, the status of

the Palestinian state as a single territorial unit will be maintained by a permanent, Safe passage between the Gaza Strip and the West Bank. The route will remain under Israeli sovereignty, but will provide for uninterrupted travel between the Gaza Strip and the West Bank by Palestinians and their visitors, as set forth in an agreed protocol.

6. The territorial arrangements in the Jerusalem area are addressed in Article VI below.

Article IV: Security

1. The Parties recognize each other's right to live in peace and security, free from war and the threat of terror and violence.

2. The Parties will refrain from the threat or use of force against each other and will ensure direct or indirect acts or threats of belligerency, hostility, subversion or violence do not originate from and are not committed within, through, or over their respective territories.

3. Israel and the Palestinian State will cooperate and coordinate their relevant security activities in order to enhance their security and the security of their citizens. This will include the establishment of a Border Security Regime (BSR) along their common borders with the aim of enforcing the rule of law and civil order, assisting in the fight against terror and violence, and regulating cross-border movement.

4. The Palestinian State [P: and Israel] will refrain from joining or in any way from assisting, promoting or cooperating with any coalition, organization or alliance with a military or security character with a third party, [P: the objective or activities of which include launching aggression or other acts of military hostility against the other party], [I: The Palestinian State and Israel will refrain from becoming party to any economic or political union or confederation or other agreement with third parties whose objectives are directed at the interests of the other party without consultations with and agreement of the other party];

5. The Palestinian State will maintain a strong police force within the context of a demilitarized state. It will not permit the stationing or presence of military forces in its territory, airspace or territorial sea except as provided for by this Agreement or as required by international law for purposes such as fulfillment of the Palestinian State's obligations under the UN Charter or law of the sea principles.

6. Israel will withdraw its forces from Palestinian territory except for specified military locations [I: and areas] in accordance with the attached map, based upon agreed modalities on their duration, size, content and provisions for access. These modalities will be designed to meet Israel's external security needs through use of minimum territory, without interfering in Palestinian internal affairs or disrupting economic or other Palestinian activities.

7. Israel will have [P: guaranteed access to] [I: control and management of] the airspace and electromagnetic spectrum in the West Bank and Gaza Strip to meet its defense needs [I: with an agreed access for Palestinian use]. Israel will provide [P: an air corridor] [I: civil flight arrangements] for Palestinian use between the Gaza Strip and the West Bank.

8. An international presence will be established to monitor and verify [I: the Palestinian demilitarization undertakings] [P: the security arrangements] set forth in this Article.

9. The Security Annex to this Agreement sets forth further details concerning the Parties' security undertakings and mechanisms for security coordination and implementation.

Article V: Refugees

1. The two sides agree on the necessity of a just settlement of the refugee problem which is a human tragedy caused by the 1947-1949 war. [P: the Palestinian refugees have the right of return in accordance with international law and natural justice to be exercised in a way that is consistent with promoting peace and implementing UNGA 194] [I: There is a need to find a comprehensive and lasting solution to the refugee problem through a concerted international effort.]

   ALT 1: The Palestinian side reiterates its insistence on the refugees' right of return in accordance with international law and natural justice. The Israeli side acknowledges the moral and material suffering caused to the Palestinian people as a result of the 1948 war and will take part in a comprehensive international effort to resolve the Palestinian refugee problem.

   ALT 2: In order to implement the provisions of relevant UN resolutions, including paragraph 11 of UNGA resolution 194, the parties agree to the programs and measures described below.

2. Given the magnitude of the refugee problem, the Parties will request the international community to establish a program to facilitate the settlement

of refugees and to provide them with compensation and rehabilitation assistance directly or indirectly through the governments of their host countries. The United States and other countries have indicated their readiness to assist in these international efforts to resolve the refugee problem.

3. As part of the international effort Israel will [I: as a matter of its sovereign discretion] facilitate phased entry of _____ refugees to its territory [P: per year on the basis of the refugees' exercise of their right of return] [I: on humanitarian grounds provided they join their families in their present place of residence in Israel, accept Israeli citizenship and waive their legal status as refugees.] In addition, in the context of pledges made by the international community, Israel will make an annual financial and/or in-kind contribution [of $_____] to the international program and/or to Palestinian efforts to deal with the refugee problem.

4. The programs and measures described in this Article will bring an end to plight of the Palestinian refugees and will fulfill the provisions of relevant UN resolutions.

5. [I: The Parties agree that a just settlement of the Israeli-Arab conflict should settle the property claims by Jewish individuals and communities due to the 1948 conflict. An international mechanism should be established to deal with these claims.]

6. The Refugee Annex to this Agreement sets forth further details concerning the agreed arrangements for addressing the refugee problem.

Article VI: Jerusalem

1. The Parties recognize the unique status of Jerusalem as a holy city for Judaism, Islam and Christianity and reaffirm their commitment to the freedom of worship and religious practice in the City.

2. The Parties are committed to enhance the status of Jerusalem as a City of Peace and to establish arrangements that will address the needs and interests of both of their citizens in the life of the City.

3. [P: The Palestinian State will have sovereignty over East Jerusalem with special arrangements for settlements, the Jewish Quarter and the Western Wall, and will provide a corridor for assured Israeli access to the Western Wall. The No-Man's Land areas will be under shared sovereignty. Therefore, on the basis of the above, Jerusalem will remain an open and undivided city.]

[I: Jerusalem will remain open and undivided, with special agreed security arrangements for the city as a whole and assured access to holy sites. The Zone of Jerusalem will consist of the territory within the municipal boundaries of Jerusalem and the adjacent Palestinian and Israeli populated areas. The Zone will consist of Israeli Territories, Palestinian Territories and areas in East Jerusalem which will be subject to Special Arrangements under Israeli sovereignty.]

4. The Jerusalem municipal area will host the national capitals of both Israel and the Palestinian State.

Articles VII: Economic Relations
Article VIII: Water
Article IX: Legal Cooperation and Law Enforcement
Article X: Coordinating Mechanisms for Implementation
Article XI: Settlement of Differences and Disputes
Article XII: Final Clauses

_____

For the Government of Israel

_____

For the Palestinian Liberation Organization
[Attachments could include, inter alia:
    Maps: Borders
        Jerusalem Area
    Annexes: Transitional Arrangements
        Security
        Refugees
        Jerusalem]

Clinton Parameters[6]

Following are the minutes of U.S. President Bill Clinton's comments at a meeting with Israeli and Palestinian representatives at the White House on December 23, 2000, as given to *Ha'aretz* by Palestinian sources.

Territory:

_____

6. *Ha'aretz*. "Clinton Minutes." December 31, 2000. Accessed through www.lexis.com (accessed October 1, 2007).

Based on what I heard, I believe that the solution should be in the mid-90 percents, between 94-96 percent of the West Bank territory of the Palestinian State.

The land annexed by Israel should be compensated by a land swap of 1-3 percent in addition to territorial arrangements such as a permanent safe passage.

The parties also should consider the swap of leased land to meet their respective needs... [this and all further ellipses in original].

The Parties should develop a map consistent with the following criteria:

- 80% of settlers in blocks

- contiguity

- Minimize the annexed areas

- Minimize the number of Palestinian [sic] affected

Security:

The key lies in an international presence that can only be withdrawn by mutual consent. This presence will also monitor the implementation of the agreement between both sides...

My best judgment is that the Israeli presence would remain in fixed locations in the Jordan Valley under the authority of the international force for another 36 months. This period could be reduced in the event of favorable regional developments that diminish the threat to Israel.

On early warning stations, Israel should maintain three facilities in the West Bank with a Palestinian liaison presence. The stations will be subject to review every 10 years with any changes in the status to be mutually agreed. (According to the Israeli version of the minutes, Clinton said the stations would be subject to review after 10 years.)

Regarding emergency developments, I understand that you will still have to develop a map of the relevant areas and routes... I propose the following definition:

Imminent and demonstrable threat to Israel's national security of a military nature that requires the activation of a national state emergency.

Of course, the international forces will need to be notified of any such determination.

On airspace, I suggest that the state of Palestine will have sovereignty over its airspace but that the two sides should work out special arrangements for Israeli training and operational needs.

I understand that the Israeli position is that Palestine should be defined as a "demilitarized state" while the Palestinian side proposes "a state with limited arms." As a compromise, I suggest calling it a "non-militarized state."

This will be consistent with the fact that in addition to a strong Palestinian security force, Palestine will have an international force for border security and deterrent purposes...

Jerusalem:

The general principle is that Arab areas are Palestinian and Jewish ones are Israeli. This would apply to the Old City as well. I urge the two sides to work on maps to create maximum contiguity for both sides.

Regarding the Haram Temple Mount, I believe that the gaps are not related to practical administration but to symbolic issues of sovereignty and to finding a way to accord respect to the religious beliefs of both sides.

I know you have been discussing a number of formulations.... I add to these two additional formulations guaranteeing Palestinian effective control over the Haram while respecting the conviction of the Jewish People. Regarding either one of those two formulations will be international monitoring to provide mutual confidence.

1. Palestinian sovereignty over the Haram and Israeli sovereignty over a) the Western Wall and the space sacred to Judaism of which it is a part or b) the Western Wall and the Holy of Holies of which it is a part.

There will be a firm commitment by both not to excavate beneath the Haram or behind the Wall.

2. Palestinian sovereignty over the Haram and Israeli sovereignty over the Western Wall and shared functional sovereignty over the issue of excavation under the Haram and behind the Wall such that mutual consent would be requested before any excavation can take place.

Refugees:

I sense that the differences are more relating to formulations and less to what will happen on a practical level.

I believe that Israel is prepared to acknowledge the moral and material suffering caused to the Palestinian people as a result of the 1948 war and the need to assist the international community in addressing the problem...

The fundamental gap is on how to handle the concept of the right of return. I know the history of the issue and how hard it will be for the Palestinian leadership to appear to be abandoning the principle.

The Israeli side could not accept any reference to a right of return that would imply a right to immigrate to Israel in defiance of Israel's sovereign policies and admission or that would threaten the Jewish character of the state.

Any solution must address both needs.

The solution will have to be consistent with the two-state approach....the state of Palestine as the homeland of the Palestinian people and the state of Israel as the homeland of the Jewish people.

Under the two-state solution, the guiding principle should be that the Palestinian state should be the focal point for the Palestinians who choose to return to the area without ruling out that Israel will accept some of these refugees.

I believe that we need to adopt a formulation on the right of return that will make clear that there is no specific right of return to Israel itself but that does not negate the aspiration of the Palestinian people to return to the area.

I propose two alternatives:

1. both sides recognize the right of Palestinian refugees to return to historic Palestine, or 2. both sides recognize the right of Palestinian refugees to return to their homeland.

The agreement will define the implementation of this general right in a way that is consistent with the two-state solution. It would list the five possible homes for the refugees:

1. The State of Palestine

2. Areas in Israel being transferred to Palestine in the land swap

3. Rehabilitation in host country

4. Resettlement in third country

5. Admission to Israel

In listing these options, the agreement will make clear that the return to the West Bank, Gaza Strip and area acquired in the land swap would be right to all Palestinian refugees, while rehabilitation in host countries, resettlement in third countries and absorption into Israel will depend upon the policies of those countries.

Israel could indicate in the agreement that it intends to establish a policy so that some the refugees would be absorbed into Israel consistent with Israel sovereign decision.

I believe that priority should be given to the refugee population in Lebanon.

The parties would agree that this implements Resolution 194.

The End of Conflict:

I propose that the agreement clearly mark the end of the conflict and its implementation put and [sic] end to all claims. This could be implemented through a UN Security Council Resolution that notes that resolutions 242 and 338 have been implemented and through the release for Palestinian prisoners.

Bush Rose Garden Speech (June 2002)[7]

For too long, the citizens of the Middle East have lived in the midst of death and fear. The hatred of a few holds the hopes of many hostage. The forces of extremism and terror are attempting to kill progress and peace by killing the innocent. And this casts a dark shadow over an entire region. For the sake of all humanity, things must change in the Middle East.

It is untenable for Israeli citizens to live in terror. It is untenable for Palestinians to live in squalor and occupation. And the current situation offers no prospect that life will improve. Israeli citizens will continue to be victimized by terrorists, and so Israel will continue to defend herself.

In the situation the Palestinian people will grow more and more miserable. My vision is two states, living side by side in peace and security. There is simply no way to achieve that peace until all parties fight terror. Yet, at this critical moment, if all parties will break with the past and set out on a new path, we can overcome the darkness with the light of hope. Peace requires a new and different Palestinian leadership, so that a Palestinian state can be born.

I call on the Palestinian people to elect new leaders, leaders not compromised by terror. I call upon them to build a practicing democracy, based on tolerance and liberty. If the Palestinian people actively pursue these goals, America and the world will actively support their efforts. If the Palestinian people meet these goals, they will be able to reach agreement with Israel and Egypt and Jordan on security and other arrangements for independence.

And when the Palestinian people have new leaders, new institutions and new security arrangements with their neighbors, the United States of America will support the creation of a Palestinian state whose borders and certain aspects of its sovereignty will be provisional until resolved as part of a final settlement in the Middle East.

---

7. White House. Office of the Press Secretary. "President Bush Calls for New Palestinian Leadership." Speech given June 24, 2002, White House Rose Garden. http://www.whitehouse.gov/news/releases/2002/06/20020624-3.html (accessed October 1, 2007).

In the work ahead, we all have responsibilities. The Palestinian people are gifted and capable, and I am confident they can achieve a new birth for their nation. A Palestinian state will never be created by terror – it will be built through reform. And reform must be more than cosmetic change, or veiled attempt to preserve the status quo. True reform will require entirely new political and economic institutions, based on democracy, market economics and action against terrorism.

Today, the elected Palestinian legislature has no authority, and power is concentrated in the hands of an unaccountable few. A Palestinian state can only serve its citizens with a new constitution which separates the powers of government. The Palestinian parliament should have the full authority of a legislative body. Local officials and government ministers need authority of their own and the independence to govern effectively.

The United States, along with the European Union and Arab states, will work with Palestinian leaders to create a new constitutional framework, and a working democracy for the Palestinian people. And the United States, along with others in the international community will help the Palestinians organize and monitor fair, multi-party local elections by the end of the year, with national elections to follow.

Today, the Palestinian people live in economic stagnation, made worse by official corruption. A Palestinian state will require a vibrant economy, where honest enterprise is encouraged by honest government. The United States, the international donor community and the World Bank stand ready to work with Palestinians on a major project of economic reform and development. The United States, the EU, the World Bank, the International Monetary Fund are willing to oversee reforms in Palestinian finances, encouraging transparency and independent auditing.

And the United States, along with our partners in the developed world, will increase our humanitarian assistance to relieve Palestinian suffering. Today, the Palestinian people lack effective courts of law and have no means to defend and vindicate their rights. A Palestinian state will require a system of reliable justice to punish those who prey on the innocent. The United States and members of the international community stand ready to work with Palestinian leaders to establish finance – establish finance and monitor a truly independent judiciary.

Today, Palestinian authorities are encouraging, not opposing, terrorism. This is unacceptable. And the United States will not support the establishment of a Palestinian state until its leaders engage in a sustained fight against the terrorists and dismantle their infrastructure. This will require an externally supervised effort to rebuild and reform the Palestinian security services. The security system must have clear lines of authority and accountability and a unified chain of command.

America is pursuing this reform along with key regional states. The world is prepared to help, yet ultimately these steps toward statehood depend on the Palestinian people and their leaders. If they energetically take the path of reform, the rewards can come quickly. If Palestinians embrace democracy, confront corruption and firmly reject terror, they can count on American support for the creation of a provisional state of Palestine.

With a dedicated effort, this state could rise rapidly, as it comes to terms with Israel, Egypt and Jordan on practical issues, such as security. The final borders, the capital and other aspects of this state's sovereignty will be negotiated between the parties, as part of a final settlement. Arab states have offered their help in this process, and their help is needed.

I've said in the past that nations are either with us or against us in the war on terror. To be counted on the side of peace, nations must act. Every leader actually committed to peace will end incitement to violence in official media, and publicly denounce homicide bombings. Every nation actually committed to peace will stop the flow of money, equipment and recruits to terrorist groups seeking the destruction of Israel – including Hamas, Islamic Jihad, and Hezbollah. Every nation actually committed to peace must block the shipment of Iranian supplies to these groups, and oppose regimes that promote terror, like Iraq. And Syria must choose the right side in the war on terror by closing terrorist camps and expelling terrorist organizations.

Leaders who want to be included in the peace process must show by their deeds an undivided support for peace. And as we move toward a peaceful solution, Arab states will be expected to build closer ties of diplomacy and commerce with Israel, leading to full normalization of relations between Israel and the entire Arab world.

Israel also has a large stake in the success of a democratic Palestine. Permanent occupation threatens Israel's identity and democracy. A stable, peaceful Palestinian state is necessary to achieve the security that Israel longs for. So I challenge Israel to take concrete steps to support the emergence of a viable, credible Palestinian state.

As we make progress towards security, Israel forces need to withdraw fully to positions they held prior to September 28, 2000. And consistent with the recommendations of the Mitchell Committee, Israeli settlement activity in the occupied territories must stop.

The Palestinian economy must be allowed to develop. As violence subsides, freedom of movement should be restored, permitting innocent Palestinians to resume work and normal life. Palestinian legislators and officials, humanitarian and international workers, must be allowed to go about the business of building a better future. And Israel should release frozen Palestinian revenues into honest, accountable hands.

I've asked Secretary Powell to work intensively with Middle Eastern and international leaders to realize the vision of a Palestinian state, focusing them on a comprehensive plan to support Palestinian reform and institution-building.

Ultimately, Israelis and Palestinians must address the core issues that divide them if there is to be a real peace, resolving all claims and ending the conflict between them. This means that the Israeli occupation that began in 1967 will be ended through a settlement negotiated between the parties, based on U.N. Resolutions 242 and 338, with Israeli withdrawal to secure and recognize borders.

We must also resolve questions concerning Jerusalem, the plight and future of Palestinian refugees, and a final peace between Israel and Lebanon, and Israel and a Syria that supports peace and fights terror.

All who are familiar with the history of the Middle East realize that there may be setbacks in this process. Trained and determined killers, as we have seen, want to stop it. Yet the Egyptian and Jordanian peace treaties with Israel remind us that with determined and responsible leadership progress can come quickly.

As new Palestinian institutions and new leaders emerge, demonstrating real performance on security and reform, I expect Israel to respond and work toward a final status agreement. With intensive effort by all, this agreement could be reached within three years from now. And I and my country will actively lead toward that goal.

I can understand the deep anger and anguish of the Israeli people. You've lived too long with fear and funerals, having to avoid markets and public transportation, and forced to put armed guards in kindergarten classrooms. The Palestinian Authority has rejected your offer at hand, and trafficked with terrorists. You have a right to a normal life; you have a right to security; and I deeply believe that you need a reformed, responsible Palestinian partner to achieve that security.

I can understand the deep anger and despair of the Palestinian people. For decades you've been treated as pawns in the Middle East conflict. Your interests have been held hostage to a comprehensive peace agreement that never seems to come, as your lives get worse year by year. You deserve democracy and the rule of law. You deserve an open society and a thriving economy. You deserve a life of hope for your children. An end to occupation and a peaceful democratic Palestinian state may seem distant, but America and our partners throughout the world stand ready to help, help you make them possible as soon as possible.

If liberty can blossom in the rocky soil of the West Bank and Gaza, it will inspire millions of men and women around the globe who are equally weary of poverty and oppression, equally entitled to the benefits of democratic government.

I have a hope for the people of Muslim countries. Your commitments to morality, and learning, and tolerance led to great historical achievements. And those values are alive in the Islamic world today. You have a rich culture, and you share the aspirations of men and women in every culture. Prosperity and freedom and dignity are not just American hopes, or Western hopes. They are universal, human hopes. And even in the violence and turmoil of the Middle East, America believes those hopes have the power to transform lives and nations.

This moment is both an opportunity and a test for all parties in the Middle East: an opportunity to lay the foundations for future peace; a test to show who is serious about peace and who is not. The choice here is stark and simple. The Bible says, "I have set before you life and death; therefore, choose life." The time has arrived for everyone in this conflict to choose peace, and hope, and life.

Thank you very much.

The Quartet's "Roadmap" Peace Plan[8]

The following is a performance-based and goal-driven roadmap, with clear phases, timelines, target dates, and benchmarks aiming at progress through reciprocal steps by the two parties in the political, security, economic, humanitarian, and institution-building fields, under the auspices of the Quartet [the United States, European Union, United Nations, and Russia]. The destination is a final and comprehensive settlement of the Israel-Palestinian conflict by 2005, as presented in President Bush's speech of 24 June, and welcomed by the EU, Russia and the

8. U.S. Department of State. Office of the Spokesman. "A Performance-Based Roadmap to a Permanent Two-State Solution to the Israeli-Palestinian Conflict." Press statement, April 30, 2003. http://www.state.gov/r/pa/prs/ps/2--3/20062.htm (accessed 10/3/07).

UN in the 16 July and 17 September Quartet Ministerial statements.

A two-state solution to the Israeli-Palestinian conflict will only be achieved through an end to violence and terrorism, when the Palestinian people have a leadership acting decisively against terror and willing and able to build a practicing democracy based on tolerance and liberty, and through Israel's readiness to do what is necessary for a democratic Palestinian state to be established, and a clear, unambiguous acceptance by both parties of the goal of a negotiated settlement as described below. The Quartet will assist and facilitate implementation of the plan, starting in Phase I, including direct discussions between the parties as required. The plan establishes a realistic timeline for implementation. However, as a performance-based plan, progress will require and depend upon the good faith efforts of the parties, and their compliance with each of the obligations outlined below. Should the parties perform their obligations rapidly, progress within and through the phases may come sooner than indicated in the plan. Non-compliance with obligations will impede progress.

A settlement, negotiated between the parties, will result in the emergence of an independent, democratic, and viable Palestinian state living side by side in peace and security with Israel and its other neighbors. The settlement will resolve the Israel-Palestinian conflict, and end the occupation that began in 1967, based on the foundations of the Madrid Conference, the principle of land for peace, UNSCRs 242, 338 and 1397, agreements previously reached by the parties, and the initiative of Saudi Crown Prince Abdullah—endorsed by the Beirut Arab League Summit—calling for acceptance of Israel as a neighbor living in peace and security, in the context of a comprehensive settlement. This initiative is a vital element of international efforts to promote a comprehensive peace on all tracks, including the Syrian-Israeli and Lebanese-Israeli tracks.

The Quartet will meet regularly at senior levels to evaluate the parties' performance on implementation of the plan. In each phase, the parties are expected to perform their obligations in parallel, unless otherwise indicated.

Phase I: Ending Terror and Violence, Normalizing Palestinian Life, and Building Palestinian Institutions — Present to May 2003

In Phase I, the Palestinians immediately undertake an unconditional cessation of violence according to the steps outlined below; such action should be accompanied by supportive measures undertaken by Israel. Palestinians and Israelis resume security cooperation based on the Tenet work plan to end violence, terrorism, and incitement through restructured and effective Palestinian security services. Palestinians undertake comprehensive political reform in preparation for statehood, including drafting a Palestinian constitution, and free, fair and open elections upon the basis of those measures. Israel takes all necessary steps to help normalize Palestinian life. Israel withdraws from Palestinian areas occupied from September 28, 2000 and the two sides restore the status quo that existed at that time, as security performance and cooperation progress. Israel also freezes all settlement activity, consistent with the Mitchell report.

At the outset of Phase I:

- Palestinian leadership issues unequivocal statement reiterating Israel's right to exist in peace and security and calling for an immediate and unconditional ceasefire to end armed activity and all acts of violence against Israelis anywhere. All official Palestinian institutions end incitement against Israel.

- Israeli leadership issues unequivocal statement affirming its commitment to the two-state vision of an independent, viable, sovereign Palestinian state living in peace and security alongside Israel, as expressed by President Bush, and calling for an immediate end to violence against Palestinians everywhere. All official Israeli institutions end incitement against Palestinians.

Security

- Palestinians declare an unequivocal end to violence and terrorism and undertake visible efforts on the ground to arrest, disrupt, and restrain individuals and groups conducting and planning violent attacks on Israelis anywhere.

- Rebuilt and refocused Palestinian Authority security apparatus begins sustained, targeted, and effective operations aimed at confronting all those engaged in terror and dismantlement of terrorist capabilities and infrastructure. This includes commencing confiscation of illegal weapons and consolidation of security authority, free of association with terror and corruption.

- GOI takes no actions undermining trust, including deportations, attacks on civilians; confiscation and/or demolition of Palestinian homes and property, as a punitive measure or to facilitate Israeli construction; destruction of Palestinian institutions and infrastructure; and other measures specified in the Tenet work plan.

- Relying on existing mechanisms and on-the-ground resources, Quartet representatives begin informal monitoring and consult with the parties on establishment of a formal monitoring mechanism and its implementation.

- Implementation, as previously agreed, of U.S. rebuilding, training and resumed security cooperation plan in collaboration with outside oversight board (U.S.–Egypt–Jordan). Quartet support for efforts to achieve a lasting, comprehensive cease-fire.

— All Palestinian security organizations are consolidated into three services reporting to an empowered Interior Minister.

— Restructured/retrained Palestinian security forces and IDF counterparts progressively resume security cooperation and other undertakings in implementation of the Tenet work plan, including regular senior-level meetings, with the participation of U.S. security officials.

- Arab states cut off public and private funding and all other forms of support for groups supporting and engaging in violence and terror.

- All donors providing budgetary support for the Palestinians channel these funds through the Palestinian Ministry of Finance's Single Treasury Account.

- As comprehensive security performance moves forward, IDF withdraws progressively from areas occupied since September 28, 2000 and the two sides restore the status quo that existed prior to September 28, 2000. Palestinian security forces redeploy to areas vacated by IDF.

Palestinian Institution-Building

- Immediate action on credible process to produce draft constitution for Palestinian statehood. As rapidly as possible, constitutional committee circulates draft Palestinian constitution, based on strong parliamentary democracy and cabinet with empowered prime minister, for public comment/debate. Constitutional committee proposes draft document for submission after elections for approval by appropriate Palestinian institutions.

- Appointment of interim prime minister or cabinet with empowered executive authority/decision-making body.

- GOI fully facilitates travel of Palestinian officials for PLC and Cabinet sessions, internationally supervised security retraining, electoral and other reform activity, and other supportive measures related to the reform efforts.

- Continued appointment of Palestinian ministers empowered to undertake fundamental reform. Completion of further steps to achieve genuine separation of powers, including any necessary Palestinian legal reforms for this purpose.

- Establishment of independent Palestinian election commission. PLC reviews and revises election law.

- Palestinian performance on judicial, administrative, and economic benchmarks, as established by the International Task Force on Palestinian Reform.

- As early as possible, and based upon the above measures and in the context of open debate and transparent candidate selection/electoral campaign based on a free, multi-party process, Palestinians hold free, open, and fair elections.

- GOI facilitates Task Force election assistance, registration of voters, movement of candidates and voting officials. Support for NGOs involved in the election process.

- GOI reopens Palestinian Chamber of Commerce and other closed Palestinian institutions in East Jerusalem based on a commitment that these institutions operate strictly in accordance with prior agreements between the parties.

Humanitarian Response

- Israel takes measures to improve the humanitarian situation. Israel and Palestinians implement in full all recommendations of the Bertini report to improve humanitarian conditions, lifting curfews and easing restrictions on movement of persons and goods, and allowing full, safe, and unfettered access of international and humanitarian personnel.

- AHLC reviews the humanitarian situation and prospects for economic development in the West Bank and Gaza and launches a major donor assistance effort, including to the reform effort.

- GOI and PA continue revenue clearance process and transfer of funds, including arrears, in accordance with agreed, transparent monitoring mechanism.

Civil Society

- Continued donor support, including increased funding through PVOs/NGOs, for people to people programs, private sector development and civil society initiatives.

Settlements

- GOI immediately dismantles settlement outposts erected since March 2001.
- Consistent with the Mitchell report, GOI freezes all settlement activity (including natural growth of settlements).

Phase II: Transition—June 2003–December 2003

In the second phase, efforts are focused on the option of creating an independent Palestinian state with provisional borders and attributes of sovereignty, based on the new constitution, as a way station to a permanent status settlement. As has been noted, this goal can be achieved when the Palestinian people have a leadership acting decisively against terror, willing and able to build a practicing democracy based on tolerance and liberty. With such a leadership, reformed civil institutions and security structures, the Palestinians will have the active support of the Quartet and the broader international community in establishing an independent, viable, state.

Progress into Phase II will be based upon the consensus judgment of the Quartet of whether conditions are appropriate to proceed, taking into account performance of both parties. Furthering and sustaining efforts to normalize Palestinian lives and build Palestinian institutions, Phase II starts after Palestinian elections and ends with possible creation of an independent Palestinian state with provisional borders in 2003. Its primary goals are continued comprehensive security performance and effective security cooperation, continued normalization of Palestinian life and institution-building, further building on and sustaining of the goals outlined in Phase I, ratification of a democratic Palestinian constitution, formal establishment of office of prime minister, consolidation of political reform, and the creation of a Palestinian state with provisional borders.

- International Conference: Convened by the Quartet, in consultation with the parties, immediately after the successful conclusion of Palestinian elections, to support Palestinian economic recovery and launch a process, leading to establishment of an independent Palestinian state with provisional borders.
  —Such a meeting would be inclusive, based on the goal of a comprehensive Middle East peace (including between Israel and Syria, and Israel and Lebanon), and based on the principles described in the preamble to this document.
  —Arab states restore pre-intifada links to Israel (trade offices, etc.).

—Revival of multilateral engagement on issues including regional water resources, environment, economic development, refugees, and arms control issues.

- New constitution for democratic, independent Palestinian state is finalized and approved by appropriate Palestinian institutions. Further elections, if required, should follow approval of the new constitution.

- Empowered reform cabinet with office of prime minister formally established, consistent with draft constitution.

- Continued comprehensive security performance, including effective security cooperation on the bases laid out in Phase I.

- Creation of an independent Palestinian state with provisional borders through a process of Israeli-Palestinian engagement, launched by the international conference. As part of this process, implementation of prior agreements, to enhance maximum territorial contiguity, including further action on settlements in conjunction with establishment of a Palestinian state with provisional borders.

- Enhanced international role in monitoring transition, with the active, sustained, and operational support of the Quartet.

- Quartet members promote international recognition of Palestinian state, including possible UN membership.

Phase III: Permanent Status Agreement and End of the Israeli-Palestinian Conflict—2004–2005

Progress into Phase III, based on consensus judgment of Quartet, and taking into account actions of both parties and Quartet monitoring. Phase III objectives are consolidation of reform and stabilization of Palestinian institutions, sustained, effective Palestinian security performance, and Israeli-Palestinian negotiations aimed at a permanent status agreement in 2005.

- Second International Conference: Convened by Quartet, in consultation with the parties, at beginning of 2004 to endorse agreement reached on an independent Palestinian state with provisional borders and formally to launch a process with the active, sustained, and operational support of the Quartet, leading to a final, permanent status resolution in 2005, including on borders, Jerusalem, refugees, settlements; and, to support progress toward a comprehensive Middle East settlement between Israel and Lebanon and Israel and Syria, to be achieved as soon as possible.

* Continued comprehensive, effective progress on the reform agenda laid out by the Task Force in preparation for final status agreement.

* Continued sustained and effective security performance, and sustained, effective security cooperation on the bases laid out in Phase I.

* International efforts to facilitate reform and stabilize Palestinian institutions and the Palestinian economy, in preparation for final status agreement.

* Parties reach final and comprehensive permanent status agreement that ends the Israel-Palestinian conflict in 2005, through a settlement negotiated between the parties based on UNSCR 242, 338, and 1397, that ends the occupation that began in 1967, and includes an agreed, just, fair, and realistic solution to the refugee issue, and a negotiated resolution on the status of Jerusalem that takes into account the political and religious concerns of both sides, and protects the religious interests of Jews, Christians, and Muslims worldwide, and fulfills the vision of two states, Israel and sovereign, independent, democratic and viable Palestine, living side-by-side in peace and security.

* Arab state acceptance of full normal relations with Israel and security for all the states of the region in the context of a comprehensive Arab-Israeli peace.

Released on April 30, 2003

Sharon-Bush Exchange of Letters (April 2004)[9]

Dear Mr. President,

The vision that you articulated in your 24 June, 2002 address constitutes one of the most significant contributions toward ensuring a bright future for the Middle East. Accordingly, the State of Israel has accepted the Roadmap, as adopted by our Government. For the first time, a practical and just formula was

9. Israeli Knesset (Sharon letter). "Letters Exchanged Between Prime Minister Ariel Sharon and President George W. Bush, April 14, 2004." http://www.knesset.gov.il/[rpcess/dcs/DisengageSharon_letters_eng.htm (accessed September 28, 2007). The White House (Bush letter). Office of the Press Secretary. "Letter From President Bush to Prime Minister Sharon." http://www.whitehouse.gov/news/releases/2004/04/20040414-3.html (accessed September 28, 2007).

presented for the achievement of peace, opening a genuine window of opportunity for progress toward a settlement between Israel and the Palestinians, involving two states living side-by-side in peace and security.

This formula sets forth the correct sequence and principles for the attainment of peace. Its full implementation represents the sole means to make genuine progress. As you have stated, a Palestinian state will never be created by terror, and Palestinians must engage in a sustained fight against the terrorists and dismantle their infrastructure. Moreover, there must be serious efforts to institute true reform and real democracy and liberty, including new leaders not compromised by terror. We are committed to this formula as the only avenue through which an agreement can be reached. We believe that this formula is the only viable one.

The Palestinian Authority under its current leadership has taken no action to meet its responsibilities under the Roadmap. Terror has not ceased, reform of the Palestinian security services has not been undertaken, and real institutional reforms have not taken place. The State of Israel continues to pay the heavy cost of constant terror. Israel must preserve its capability to protect itself and deter its enemies, and we thus retain our right to defend ourselves against terrorism and to take actions against terrorist organizations.

Having reached the conclusion that, for the time being, there exists no Palestinian partner with whom to advance peacefully toward a settlement and since the current impasse is unhelpful to the achievement of our shared goals, I have decided to initiate a process of gradual disengagement with the hope of reducing friction between Israelis and Palestinians. The Disengagement Plan is designed to improve security for Israel and stabilize our political and economic situation. It will enable us to deploy our forces more effectively until such time that conditions in the Palestinian Authority allow for the full implementation of the Roadmap to resume.

I attach, for your review, the main principles of the Disengagement Plan. This initiative, which we are not undertaking under the Roadmap, represents an independent Israeli plan, yet is not inconsistent with the Roadmap. According to this plan, the State of Israel intends to relocate military installations and all Israeli villages and towns in the Gaza Strip, as well as other military installations and a small number of villages in Samaria.

In this context, we also plan to accelerate construction of the Security Fence, whose completion is essential in order to ensure the security of the citizens of Israel. The fence is a security rather than political barrier, temporary rather than permanent, and therefore will not prejudice any final status issues including final borders. The route of the Fence, as approved by our Government's decisions, will take into account, consistent with security needs, its impact on Palestinians not engaged in terrorist activities.

Upon my return from Washington, I expect to submit this Plan for the approval of the Cabinet and the Knesset, and I firmly believe that it will win such approval.

The Disengagement Plan will create a new and better reality for the State of Israel, enhance its security and economy, and strengthen the fortitude of its people. In this context, I believe it is important to bring new opportunities to the Negev and the Galilee. Additionally, the Plan will entail a series of measures with the inherent potential to improve the lot of the Palestinian Authority, providing that it demonstrates the wisdom to take advantage of this opportunity. The execution of the Disengagement Plan holds the prospect of stimulating positive changes within the Palestinian Authority that might create the necessary conditions for the resumption of direct negotiations.

We view the achievement of a settlement between Israel and the Palestinians as our central focus and are committed to realizing this objective. Progress toward this goal must be anchored exclusively in the Roadmap and we will oppose any other plan.

In this regard, we are fully aware of the responsibilities facing the State of Israel. These include limitations on the growth of settlements; removal of unauthorized outposts; and steps to increase, to the extent permitted by security needs, freedom of movement for Palestinians not engaged in terrorism. Under separate cover we are sending to you a full description of the steps the State of Israel is taking to meet all its responsibilities.

The Government of Israel supports the United States' efforts to reform the Palestinian security services to meet their Roadmap obligations to fight terror. Israel also supports the American's efforts, working with the international community, to promote the reform process, build institutions and improve the economy of the Palestinian Authority and to enhance the welfare of its people, in the hope that a new Palestinian leadership will prove able to fulfill its obligations under the Roadmap.

I want to again express my appreciation for your courageous leadership in the war against global terror, your important initiative to revitalize the Middle East as a more fitting home for its people and, primarily, your personal friendship and profound support for the State of Israel.

Sincerely,
Ariel Sharon

April 14, 2004

His Excellency
Ariel Sharon
Prime Minister of Israel

Dear Mr. Prime Minister:

Thank you for your letter setting out your disengagement plan.

The United States remains hopeful and determined to find a way forward toward a resolution of the Israeli-Palestinian dispute. I remain committed to my June 24, 2002 vision of two states living side by side in peace and security as the key to peace, and to the roadmap as the route to get there.

We welcome the disengagement plan you have prepared, under which Israel would withdraw certain military installations and all settlements from Gaza, and withdraw certain military installations and settlements in the West Bank. These steps described in the plan will mark real progress toward realizing my June 24, 2002 vision, and make a real contribution towards peace. We also understand that, in this context, Israel believes it is important to bring new opportunities to the Negev and the Galilee. We are hopeful that steps pursuant to this plan, consistent with my vision, will remind all states and parties of their own obligations under the roadmap.

The United States appreciates the risks such an undertaking represents. I therefore want to reassure you on several points.

First, the United States remains committed to my vision and to its implementation as described in the roadmap. The United States will do its utmost to prevent any attempt by anyone to impose any other plan. Under the roadmap, Palestinians must undertake an immediate cessation of armed activity and all acts of violence against Israelis anywhere, and all official Palestinian institutions must end incitement against Israel. The Palestinian leadership must act decisively against terror, including sustained, targeted, and effective operations to stop terrorism and dismantle terrorist capabilities and infrastructure. Palestinians must undertake a comprehensive and fundamental political reform that includes a strong parliamentary democracy and an empowered prime minister.

Second, there will be no security for Israelis or Palestinians until they and all states, in the region and beyond, join together to fight terrorism and dismantle terrorist organizations. The United States reiterates its steadfast commitment to Israel's security, including secure, defensible borders, and to preserve and strengthen Israel's capability to deter and defend itself, by itself, against any threat or possible combination of threats.

Third, Israel will retain its right to defend itself against terrorism, including to take actions against terrorist organizations. The United States will lead efforts, working together with Jordan, Egypt, and others in the international community, to build the capacity and will of Palestinian institutions to fight terrorism, dismantle terrorist organizations, and prevent the areas from which Israel has withdrawn from posing a threat that would have to be addressed by any other means. The United States understands that after Israel withdraws from Gaza and/or parts of the West Bank, and pending agreements on other arrangements, existing arrangements regarding control of airspace, territorial waters, and land passages of the West Bank and Gaza will continue. The United States is strongly committed to Israel's security and well-being as a Jewish state. It seems clear that an agreed, just, fair, and realistic framework for a solution to the Palestinian refugee issue as part of any final status agreement will need to be found through the establishment of a Palestinian state, and the settling of Palestinian refugees there, rather than in Israel.

As part of a final peace settlement, Israel must have secure and recognized borders, which should emerge from negotiations between the parties in accordance with UNSC Resolutions 242 and 338. In light of new realities on the ground, including already existing major Israeli populations centers, it is unrealistic to expect that the outcome of final status negotiations will be a full and complete return to the armistice lines of 1949, and all previous efforts to negotiate a two-state solution have reached the same conclusion. It is realistic to expect that any final status agreement will only be achieved on the basis of mutually agreed changes that reflect these realities.

I know that, as you state in your letter, you are aware that certain responsibilities face the State of Israel. Among these, your government has stated that the barrier being erected by Israel should be a security rather than political barrier, should be temporary rather than permanent, and therefore not prejudice any final status issues including final borders, and its route should take into account, consistent with security needs, its impact on Palestinians not engaged in terrorist activities.

As you know, the United States supports the establishment of a Palestinian state that is viable, contiguous, sovereign, and independent, so that the Palestinian people can build their own future in accordance with my vision set forth in June 2002 and with the path set forth in the roadmap. The United States will join with others in the international community to foster the development of democratic political institutions and new leadership committed to those institutions, the reconstruction of civic institutions, the growth of a free and prosperous economy, and the building of capable security institutions dedicated to maintaining law and order and dismantling terrorist organizations.

A peace settlement negotiated between Israelis and Palestinians would be a great boon not only to those peoples but to the peoples of the entire region. Accordingly, the United States believes that all states in the region have special responsibilities: to support the building of the institutions of a Palestinian state; to fight terrorism, and cut off all forms of assistance to individuals and groups engaged in terrorism; and to begin now to move toward more normal relations with the State of Israel. These actions would be true contributions to building peace in the region.

Mr. Prime Minister, you have described a bold and historic initiative that can make an important contribution to peace. I commend your efforts and your courageous decision which I support. As a close friend and ally, the United States intends to work closely with you to help make it a success.

Sincerely,
George W. Bush

Letter from Dov Weissglas to Condoleezza Rice (April 2004)[10]

Dr. Condoleezza Rice
National Security Adviser
The White House
Washington, D.C.

Dear Dr. Rice,

On behalf of the Prime Minister of the State of Israel, Mr. Ariel Sharon, I wish to reconfirm the following understanding, which had been reached between us:

1. Restrictions on settlement growth: within the agreed principles of settlement activities, an effort will be made in the next few days to have a better definition of the construction line of settlements in Judea and Samaria [the West Bank]. An Israeli team, in conjunction with Ambassador Kurtzer, will review aerial photos of settlements and will jointly define the construction line of each of the settlements.

2. Removal of unauthorized outposts: the Prime Minister and the Minister of defense, jointly, will prepare a list of unauthorized outposts with indicative dates of their removal; the Israeli Defense forces and/or the Israeli Police will take continuous action to remove those outposts in the targeted dates. The said list will be presented to Ambassador Kurtzer within 30 days.

3. Mobility restrictions in Judea & Samaria: the Minister of Defense will provide Ambassador Kurtzer with a map indicating roadblocks and other transportational barriers posed across Judea & Samaria. A list of barriers already removed and a timetable for further removals will be included in this list. Needless to say, the matter of the existence of transportational barriers fully depends on the current security situation and might be changed accordingly.

4. Legal attachments of Palestinian revenues: the matter is pending in various courts of law in Israel, awaiting judicial decisions. We will urge the State Attorney's office to take any possible legal measure to expedite the rendering of those decisions.

5. The Government of Israel extends to the Government of the United States the following assurances:

---

10. Israeli Ministry of Foreign Affairs. "Letter from Dov Weissglas, Chief of the PM's Bureau, to National Security Adviser, Dr. Condoleezza Rice," April 18, 2004. http://www.mfa.gov.il/MFA/Peace+Process/Reference+Documents/Letter+Weissglas-Rice+18-Apr-2004.htm (accessed on November 1, 2007).

a. The Israeli government remains committed to the two-state solution—Israel and Palestine living side by side in peace and security—as the key to peace in the Middle East.

b. The Israeli government remains committed to the Roadmap as the only route to achieving the two-state solution.

c. The Israeli government believes that its disengagement plan and related steps on the West Bank concerning settlement growth, unauthorized outposts, and easing of restrictions on the movement of Palestinians not engaged in terror are consistent with the Roadmap and, in many cases, are steps actually called for in certain phases of the Roadmap.

d. The Israeli government believes that further steps by it, even if consistent with the Roadmap, cannot be taken absent the emergence of a Palestinian partner committed to peace, democratic reform, and the fight against terror.

e. Once such a Palestinian partner emerges, the Israeli government will perform its obligations, as called for in the Roadmap, as part of the performance-based plan set out in the Roadmap for reaching a negotiated final status agreement.

f. The Israeli government remains committed to the negotiation between the parties of a final status resolution of all outstanding issues.

g. The Government of Israel supports the United States' efforts to reform the Palestinian security services to meet their Roadmap obligations to fight terror. Israel also supports the American efforts, working with the international community, to promote the reform process, build institutions, and improve the economy of the Palestinian Authority and to enhance the welfare of its people, in the hope that a new Palestinian leadership will prove able to fulfill its obligations under the Roadmap. The Israeli Government will take all reasonable actions requested by these parties to facilitate these efforts.

h. As the Government of Israel has stated, the barrier being erected by Israel should be a security rather than a political barrier, should be temporary rather than permanent, and therefore not prejudice any final status issues including final borders, and its route should take into account, consistent with security needs, its impact on Palestinians not engaged in terrorist activities.

Sincerely,

Dov Weissglas
Chief of the Prime Minister's Bureau

Israeli-Palestinian "Joint Understanding" (Presented by President Bush at Annapolis Conference, November 27, 2007)[11]

The representatives of the government of the state of Israel and the Palestinian Liberation Organization, represented respective by Prime Minister Ehud Olmert, and President Mahmoud Abbas in his capacity as Chairman of the PLO Executive Committee and President of the Palestinian Authority, have convened in Annapolis, Maryland, under the auspices of President George W. Bush of the United States of America, and with the support of the participants of this international conference, having concluded the following joint understanding.

We express our determination to bring an end to bloodshed, suffering and decades of conflict between our peoples; to usher in a new era of peace, based on freedom, security, justice, dignity, respect and mutual recognition; to propagate a culture of peace and nonviolence; to confront terrorism and incitement, whether committed by Palestinians or Israelis. In furtherance of the goal of two states, Israel and Palestine, living side by side in peace and security, we agree to immediately launch good-faith bilateral negotiations in order to conclude a peace treaty, resolving all outstanding issues, including all core issues without exception, as specified in previous agreements.

We agree to engage in vigorous, ongoing and continuous negotiations, and shall make every effort to conclude an agreement before the end of 2008. For this purpose, a steering committee, led jointly by the head of the delegation of each party, will meet continuously, as agreed. The steering committee will develop a joint work plan and establish and oversee the work of negotiations teams to address all issues, to be headed by one lead representative from each party. The first session of the steering committee will be held on 12 December 2007.

President Abbas and Prime Minister Olmert will continue to meet on a biweekly basis to follow up the negotiations in order to offer all necessary assistance for their advancement.

The parties also commit to immediately implement their respective obligations under the performance-based road map to a permanent two-state solution

---

11. White House. Office of the Press Secretary. "Joint Understanding" Read by President Bush at Annapolis Conference." http://www.state.gov/p/nea/ris/95696.htm (accessed December 17, 2007).

to the Israel-Palestinian conflict, issued by the Quartet on 30 April 2003—this is called the road map—and agree to form an American, Palestinian and Israeli mechanism, led by the United States, to follow up on the implementation of the road map.

The parties further commit to continue the implementation of the ongoing obligations of the road map until they reach a peace treaty. The United States will monitor and judge the fulfillment of the commitment of both sides of the road map. Unless otherwise agreed by the parties, implementation of the future peace treaty will be subject to the implementation of the road map, as judged by the United States.

Online Documents and Primary Sources

The following documents and those in the preceding section can be accessed on this book's Web page at www.usip.org:

- The Madrid Conference: U.S. Letters of Assurance, October, 18, 1991
- Annexes of the Declaration of Principles on Interim Self-Government Arrangements (the "Oslo Accord"), September 13, 1993
- The Interim Agreement ("Oslo II"), September 28, 1995
- The Hebron Accord, January 1997
- Note for the Record, January 15, 1997
- Letter from Secretary of State Warren Christopher to Israeli Prime Minister Netanyahu
- Timeline Annex of the Wye River Memorandum, October 23, 1998
- The "Moratinos Report" on the Israeli-Palestinian Talks at Taba, January 2001
- Report of the Sharm el-Sheikh Fact-Finding Committee (the "Mitchell Report"), April 30, 2001
- Tenet Ceasefire Agreement, June 13, 2001
- Second U.S. "Joint Goals" Proposal (the "Zinni Paper"), March 26, 2002
- Arab League Peace Initiative (the "Beirut Declaration"), March 28, 2002
- Nusseibeh-Ayalon Initiative, July 2002
- Agreement on Movement and Access, November 15, 2005
- Agreed Principles on Rafah Crossing, November 15, 2005
- Quartet Statement following Hamas victory in Palestinian legislative elections, January 30, 2006
- President Bush's Speech at Annapolis, November 27, 2007

RECOMMENDED READINGS

Abbas, Mahmoud (Abu Mazen). *Through Secret Channels: The Road to Oslo.* Reading: Garnet Publishing, 1995.

Abu-Amr, Ziad. "The Significance of Jerusalem: A Muslim Perspective." *Palestine-Israel Journal* 2, no. 2 (1995): 23–31.

Abu Odeh, Adnan. "Two Capitals in an Undivided Jerusalem." *Foreign Affairs* 71, no. 2 (Spring 1992): 183.

———. *Jordanians, Palestinians, and the Hashemite Kingdom in the Middle East Peace Process.* Washington, DC: United States Institute of Peace Press, 1999.

Agha, Hussein, and Ahmad S. Khalidi. *A Framework for a Palestinian National Security Doctrine.* London: Chatham House, 2006.

Agha, Hussein, and Robert Malley. "Camp David and After: An Exchange (A Reply to Ehud Barak)." *The New York Review of Books,* June 13, 2002.

———. "Camp David: The Tragedy of Errors." *The New York Review of Books,* August 9, 2001.

Albin, Cecilia. "Explaining Conflict Transformation: How Jerusalem Became Negotiable." *Cambridge Review of International Affairs* 18, no. 3 (October 2005): 339–355.

———. "Negotiating Intractable Conflicts: On the Future of Jerusalem." *Cooperation and Conflict* 32, no. 1 (1997): 29–77.

Al-Moualem, Walid. "Fresh Light on the Syrian-Israeli Peace Negotiations: An Interview with Ambassador Walid Al-Moualem." *Journal of Palestine Studies* 26, no. 2 (Winter 1997): 81–94.

Alpher, Yossi. *The Future of the Israeli-Palestinian Conflict: Critical Trends Affecting Israel.* Special Report no. 149. Washington, DC: United States Institute of Peace Press, 2005.

Aly, Abdel Moneim Said, and Shai Feldman. *Ecopolitics: Changing the Regional Context of Arab-Israeli Peacemaking.* Cambridge, MA: Belfer Center for Science and International Affairs, 2003.

Arens, Moshe. *Broken Covenant: American Foreign Policy and the Crisis between the U.S. and Israel.* New York: Simon & Schuster, 1995.

Arieli, Shaul. "They Just Can't Hear Each Other." Interview by Akiva Eldar. *Haaretz,* March 11, 2003.

————. "Toward a Final Settlement in Jerusalem: Redefinition Rather than Partition." *Jaffee Center Strategic Assessment* 8, no. 1 (June 2005). www.tau.ac.il/jcss/sa/v8n1p5Arieli. html (accessed October 30, 2007).

Ashrawi, Hanan. *This Side of Peace: A Personal Account.* New York: Simon & Schuster, 1995.

Baker, James A., III. *The Politics of Diplomacy: Revolution, War & Peace, 1989–1992.* New York: G.P. Putnam's Sons, 1995.

Baker, James A., III, and Lee H. Hamilton, co-chairs. *The Iraq Study Group Report.* New York: Vintage Books, 2006.

Bar-On, Mordechai. *In Pursuit of Peace: A History of the Israeli Peace Movement.* Washington, DC: United States Institute of Peace Press, 1996.

Barnea, Nahum, and Ariel Kastner. *Backchannel: Bush, Sharon and the Uses of Unilateralism.* Saban Center Monograph Series no. 2. Washington, DC: Brookings Institution, 2006.

Ben-Ami, Shlomo. *Scars of War, Wounds of Peace.* New York: Oxford University Press, 2006.

————. "So Close and Yet So Far: Lessons from the Israeli-Palestinian Peace Process." *Israel Studies* 10, no. 2 (Summer 2005): 72–90.

Blumenfeld, Laura. "Three Peace Suits: For These Passionate American Diplomats, a Middle East Settlement Is the Goal of a Lifetime." *The Washington Post,* February 24, 1997.

Blumenthal, Sidney. "The Western Front." *The New Yorker,* June 5, 1995.

Bouillon, Markus E. "The Middle East: Fragility and Crisis." Coping with Crisis Working Paper Series. New York: International Peace Academy, 2007.

Boutros-Ghali, Boutros. *Egypt's Road to Jerusalem: A Diplomat's Story of the Struggle for Peace in the Middle East.* New York: Random House, 1997.

Brom, Shlomo. "From Rejection to Acceptance: Israeli National Security Thinking and Palestinian Statehood." Special Report no. 177. Washington, DC: United States Institute of Peace Press, 2007.

Brynen, Rex. *A Very Political Economy.* Washington, DC: United States Institute of Peace Press, 2000.

Clawson, Patrick, and Zoe Danon Gedal. *Dollars and Diplomacy: The Impact of U.S. Economic Initiatives on Arab-Israeli Negotiations.* Policy Papers no. 49. Washington, DC: Washington Institute for Near East Policy, January 1999.

Clinton, William J. *My Life.* New York: Knopf, 2004.

Cobban, Helena. *The Israeli-Syrian Peace Talks: 1991–96 and Beyond.* Washington, DC: United States Institute of Peace Press, 1999.

Cohen, Stephen Philip. *Foundations for a Future Peace: Ten Principles for Mideast Peacemaking.* Report of the IPF Study Group. Washington, DC: Israel Policy Forum, 2002.

Daoudi, Riad. "Remarks on Syria-Israel Negotiations." Delivered at the Madrid +15 Conference, Madrid, Spain, January 12, 2007.

Eisenberg, Laura Zittrain, and Neil Caplan. "The Israel-Jordan Peace Treaty: Patterns of Negotiation, Problems of Implementation." *Israel Affairs* 9, no. 3 (Spring 2003): 87–110.

Enderlin, Charles. *Shattered Dreams: The Failure of the Peace Process in the Middle East, 1995–2002.* Translated by Susan Fairfield. New York: Other Press, 2003.

Gazit, Shlomo. *Trapped Fools: Thirty Years of Israeli Policy in the Territories.* London: Frank Cass, 2003.

George, Alexander. *Forceful Persuasion: Coercive Diplomacy as an Alternative to War.* Washington, DC: United States Institute of Peace Press, 1991.

Golan, Galia. *Israel and Palestine: Peace Plans from Oslo to Disengagement.* Princeton: Markus Wiener Publishers, 2007.

Goldberg, J.J. *Jewish Power: Inside the American Jewish Establishment.* Reading, MA: Addison-Wesley Publishing Co., 1996.

Hanieh, Akram. "The Camp David Papers." *Journal of Palestine Studies* 30, no. 2 (Winter 2001): 75–97.

Hof, Frederic C. *Line of Battle, Border of Peace? The Line of June 4, 1967.* Washington, DC: Middle East Insight, 1999.

Hof, Frederic C., Samuel Lewis, Robert Pelletreau, Jr., Thomas Pickering, Steven L. Spiegel, and Edward S. Walker. "A Guide to a Successful November International Conference." *Israel Policy Forum Focus,* October 10, 2007. www.israelpolicyforum.org (accessed October 28, 2007).

Hroub, Khaled. *Hamas: Political Thought and Practice.* Washington, DC: Institute for Palestine Studies, 2000.

Indyk, Martin, Robert Malley, Aaron David Miller, and Dennis Ross. "Lessons of Arab-Israeli Negotiating: Four Negotiators Look Back and Ahead." Proceedings of Middle East Institute conference entitled "Lessons of Arab-Israeli Negotiating: Four Negotiators Look Back and Ahead." Washington, DC, April 25, 2005. www.mideasti.org (accessed October 30, 2007).

Israeli, Raphael. "Armistice in Jerusalem: Once Again?" *Israel Affairs* 10, no. 3 (Spring 2004): 74–89.

Kacowicz, Arie M. "Rashomon in Jerusalem: Mapping the Israeli Negotiators' Positions on the Israeli-Palestinian Peace Process, 1993–2001." *International Studies Perspectives* 6, no. 2 (May 2005): 252–273.

Khalidi, Rashid. *The Iron Cage: The Story of the Palestinian Struggle for Statehood.* Boston: Beacon Press, 2006.

Kimmerling, Baruch, and Joel S. Migdal. *The Palestinian People: A History.* Cambridge, MA: Harvard University Press, 2003.

Klein, Menachem. *The Jerusalem Problem: The Struggle for Permanent Status.* Gainesville: University Press of Florida, 2003.

Kurtzer, Daniel C. "Intifada III: Coming Soon to a TV Screen Near You." *The American Interest* 3, no. 2 (January/February 2007): 108–114.

————. "The U.S. Must Get Tough in Promoting Arab-Israeli Peace Efforts." *Palestine Israel Journal* 13, no. 4 (2007): 20–24.

————. "Madrid, Oslo and the Middle East Road Map: Opportunities Squandered." Keynote address delivered to the Annual Meeting of the Association for Israel Studies, Banff, Canada, May 29, 2006.

Laschet, Armin. "Working Group on Budgetary Assistance to the Palestinian Authority: Draft Conclusions." Brussels: European Union, n.d. [2004]. www.eufunding.org/accountability/DraftConclusionsLaschet.pdf (accessed October 28, 2007).

Lasensky, Scott. "Dollarizing Peace: Nixon, Kissinger, and the Creation of the US-Israeli Alliance." *Israel Affairs* 13, no. 1 (January 2007): 164–186.

————. "Paying for Peace: The Oslo Process and the Limits of U.S. Foreign Aid." *Middle East Journal* 58, no. 2 (Spring 2004): 210–234.

Lasensky, Scott, and Robert Grace. *Dollars and Diplomacy: Foreign Aid and the Palestinian Question*. USIPeace Briefing. Washington, DC: United States Institute of Peace, 2006. www.usip.org (accessed October 28, 2007).

Levitt, Matthew. *Hamas: Politics, Charity, and Terrorism in the Service of Jihad*. New Haven: Yale University Press, 2006.

Levy, Daniel, Ghaith al-Omari, and Robert Malley. "Ten Commandments for Mideast Peace." *The American Prospect*, May 20, 2007.

Lewis, Samuel, and Kenneth W. Stein. *Making Peace among Arabs and Israelis: Lessons from Fifty Years of Negotiating Experience*. Washington, DC: United States Institute of Peace Press, 1991.

Makovsky, David. *Engagement through Disengagement: Gaza and the Potential for Renewed Israeli-Palestinian Peacemaking*. Washington, DC: Washington Institute for Near East Policy, 2005.

————. *Making Peace with the PLO: The Rabin Government's Road to the Oslo Accord*. Boulder, CO: Westview Press, 1996.

Makovsky, David, Robert Malley, and Steven Spiegel. "Arab-Israeli Futures: Next Steps for the United States." Paper presented at Pathways to Peace: The United States and the Middle East Peace Process, Washington, DC, January 27, 2005. www.usip.org (October 24, 2007).

Malley, Robert. "A New Middle East." *The New York Review of Books,* September 21, 2006.

Miller, Aaron David. *America and the Much Too Promised Land: The Elusive Search for Arab-Israeli Peace*. New York: Bantam Dell, forthcoming (2008).

————. "The Pursuit of Arab-Israeli Peace, 1993–2000: Where Did the U.S. Go Wrong?" Speech delivered at Tel Aviv University, May 3, 2004.

Mishal, Shaul, and Avraham Sela. *The Palestinian Hamas: Vision, Violence, and Coexistence*. New York: Columbia University Press, 2000.

Moratinos, Miguel Angel. "Moratinos' 'Non-Paper' on Taba Negotiations." United Nations

Information System on the Question of Palestine, January 27, 2001. www.un.org (accessed October 24, 2007).

Morris, Benny. *Righteous Victims: A History of the Zionist-Arab Conflict, 1881–2001*. New York: Vintage Books, 1999.

Muasher, Marwan. *The Arab Center: Moderation and the Search for Peace in the Middle East*. New Haven: Yale University Press, forthcoming (2008).

Palestinian Authority (PA). "First Annual Report 1996." Public Monitoring Department, Gaza, May 1997.

Palestinian Liberation Organization (PLO) Negotiation Affairs Department. "Memorandum: Lessons Learned Concerning U.S. Involvement in the Palestinian-Israeli Peace Process over the Last Seven Years." Released by the Palestinian negotiating team, January 20, 2001.

Peri, Yoram. *Generals in the Cabinet Room: How the Military Shapes Israeli Policy*. Washington, DC: United States Institute of Peace Press, 2006.

Pressman, Jeremy. "The Second Intifada: Background and Causes of the Israeli-Palestinian Conflict." *The Journal of Conflict Studies* (Fall 2003): 114–141.

———. *The United States and the Israel-Hezbollah War*. Middle East Brief no. 13. Waltham, MA: Crown Center for Middle East Studies, 2006.

———. "Visions in Collision: What Happened at Camp David and Taba?" *International Security* 28, no. 2 (Fall 2003): 5–43.

Quandt, William B. "Clinton and the Arab-Israeli Conflict: The Limits of Incrementalism." *Journal of Palestine Studies* 30, no. 2 (Winter 2001): 26–40.

———. *Peace Process: American Diplomacy and the Arab-Israeli Conflict since 1967*, 3rd ed. Washington, DC, and Berkeley, CA: Brookings Institution Press and University of California Press, 2005.

Qurei, Ahmed (Abu Ala). *From Oslo to Jerusalem: The Palestinian Story of the Secret Negotiations*. London: I.B. Tauris, 2006.

Rabin, Yitzhak. *The Rabin Memoirs*. Boston: Little, Brown and Company, 1979.

Rabinovich, Itamar. *The Brink of Peace: The Israeli-Syrian Negotiations*. Princeton: Princeton University Press, 1998.

———. *Waging Peace: Israel and the Arabs at the End of the Century*. New York: Farrar, Straus and Giroux, 1999.

———. and Jehuda Reinharz. *Israel in the Middle East*. 2nd ed. Waltham, MA: Brandeis University Press, 2007.

RAND Corporation. *Building a Successful Palestinian State*. Palestinian State Study Team. Santa Monica, CA: The RAND Corporation, 2005.

Riêdel, Bruce. "Camp David—The US-Israeli Bargain." Bitterlemons.org, July 15, 2002, edition 26. www.bitterlemons.org (accessed October 28, 2007).

Robinson, Glenn. "Palestine After Arafat." *The Washington Quarterly* 23, no. 4 (2000): 77–90.

Rocard, Michel, and Henry Siegman. *Strengthening Palestinian Public Institutions.* Task Force Report, no. 22. New York: Council on Foreign Relations Press, 1999.

Ross, Dennis. "Taking Stock: The Bush Administration and the Roadmap to Peace." *The National Interest* 73 (Fall 2003): 11.

———. *The Missing Peace: The Inside Story of the Fight for Middle East Peace.* New York: Farrar, Straus and Giroux, 2004.

Ross, Dennis, Margaret Warner, and Jim Hoagland. 2001. "From Oslo to Camp David to Taba: Setting the Record Straight." Transcript of a question-and-answer session at the Washington Institute for Near East Policy, Washington, DC, August 8. www.washingtoninstitute.org (accessed October 31, 2007).

Sachar, Howard M. *A History of Israel: From the Rise of Zionism to Our Time,* 3rd ed. New York: Knopf, 2007.

Said, Edward W. *Peace and Its Discontents: Essays on Palestine in the Middle East Peace Process.* New York: Vintage, 1996.

Sasson, Talya. "Summary of the Opinion Concerning Unauthorized Outposts." Israel Ministry of Foreign Affairs, March 10, 2005. www.mfa.gov (accessed October 28, 2007).

Saunders, Harold H. *The Other Walls: The Arab-Israeli Peace Process.* Princeton, NJ: Princeton University Press, 1985.

Savir, Uri. *The Process: 1,100 Days that Changed the Middle East.* New York: Random House, 1998.

Sayigh, Yezid. *Armed Struggle and the Search for State: The Palestinian National Movement, 1949–1993.* Oxford: Oxford University Press, 2000.

———. "Arafat and the Anatomy of a Revolt." *Survival* 43, no. 3 (Autumn 2001): 47–60.

Seale, Patrick. "The Syria-Israel Negotiations: Who is Telling the Truth?" *Journal of Palestine Studies* 29, no. 2 (Winter 2000): 65–77.

Shamir, Shimon, and Bruce Maddy-Weitzman, eds. *The Camp David Summit: What Went Wrong.* Brighton, UK: Sussex Academic Press, 2005.

Shamir, Yitzhak. *Summing Up: An Autobiography,* 1st American ed. New York: Little, Brown, 1994.

Shavit, Ari. "End of a Journey: Conversation with Shlomo Ben-Ami." *Ha'aretz,* September 14, 2001.

Sher, Gilead. *Within Reach: The Israeli-Palestinian Peace Negotiations, 1999–2001.* London: Routledge, 2006.

Shikaki, Khalil. "The Politics of Paralysis II: Peace Now or Hamas Later." *Foreign Affairs* 77, no. 4 (July/August 1998): 29–43.

———. "Palestinians Divided." *Foreign Affairs* 81, no. 1 (January/February 2002): 89–105.

————. *Willing to Compromise: Palestinian Public Opinion and the Peace Process.* Special Report no. 158. Washington, DC: United States Institute of Peace Press, 2006.

Shultz, George P. *Turmoil and Triumph: My Years as Secretary of State.* New York: Charles Scribner's Sons, 1993.

Singer, Saul. "American Evenhandedness in the Mideast Peace Process: Lessons from Camp David II and the Al-Aqsa Intifada." *Jerusalem Letter* 444, December 15, 2000. www.jcpa.org (accessed October 28, 2007).

Slater, Jerome. "What Went Wrong? The Collapse of the Israeli-Palestinian Peace Process." *Political Science Quarterly* 116, no. 2 (Summer 2001): 171–199.

————. "Lost Opportunities for Peace in the Arab-Israeli Conflict: Israel and Syria, 1948–2001." *International Security* 27, no. 1 (Summer 2002): 79–106.

Smith, Charles D. *Palestine and the Arab Israeli Conflict: A History with Documents,* 6th ed. New York: Palgrave Macmillan, 2007.

Sontag, Susan. "Quest for Mideast Peace: How and Why It Failed." *New York Times*, July 26, 2001.

Spiegel, Steven. *The Other Arab-Israeli Conflict: Making America's Middle East Policy, from Truman to Reagan.* Chicago: The University of Chicago Press, 1985.

————. "Neighborhood Watch." *Democracy Journal* 4 (Spring 2007): 59–73.

Swisher, Clayton E. "Investigating Blame: U.S. Mediation of the Arab-Israeli Conflict from 1999 to 2001." Master's thesis, Georgetown University, 2003.

————. *The Truth about Camp David: The Untold Story about the Collapse of the Middle East Peace Process.* New York: Nation Books, 2004.

Telhami, Shibley. *Power and Leadership in International Bargaining: The Path to the Camp David Accords.* New York: Columbia University Press, 1990.

————. "Camp David II: Assumptions and Consequences." *Current History* 100, no. 642 (January 2001): 10–14.

————. *The Stakes: America and the Middle East—The Consequences of Power and the Choice for Peace.* Boulder, CO: Westview Press, 2002.

United States Institute of Peace. "U.S. Negotiating Behavior." Special Report no. 94. Washington, DC: United States Institute of Peace Press, 2002.

Wasserstein, Bernard. *Divided Jerusalem.* New Haven: Yale University Press, 2001.

Waxman, Dov. "Israel's Dilemma: Unity or Peace?" *Israel Affairs* 12, no. 2 (April 2006): 195–220.

————. *The Pursuit of Peace and the Crisis of Israeli Identity.* New York: Palgrave Macmillan, 2006.

Wittes, Tamara Cofman, ed. *How Israelis and Palestinians Negotiate: A Cross-Cultural Analysis of the Oslo Peace Process.* Washington, DC: United States Institute of Peace Press, 2005.

United States Institute of Peace

The United States Institute of Peace is an independent, nonpartisan, national institution established and funded by Congress. Its goals are to help prevent and resolve violent conflicts, promote post-conflict stability and development, and increase peacebuilding capacity, tools, and intellectual capital worldwide. The Institute does this by empowering others with knowledge, skills, and resources, as well as by directly engaging in peacebuilding efforts around the globe.

Chairman of the Board: J. Robinson West
Vice Chairman: María Otero
President: Richard H. Solomon
Executive Vice President: Patricia Powers Thomson
Vice President: Charles E. Nelson

Board of Directors

J. ROBINSON WEST (Chair), Chairman, PFC Energy, Washington, D.C.

MARÍA OTERO (Vice Chairman), President, ACCION International, Boston, Mass.

HOLLY J. BURKHALTER, Vice President, Government Affairs, International Justice Mission, Washington, D.C.

ANNE H. CAHN, Former Scholar in Residence, American University, Washington, D.C.

CHESTER A. CROCKER, James R. Schlesinger Professor of Strategic Studies, School of Foreign Service, Georgetown University, Washington, D.C.

LAURIE S. FULTON, Partner, Williams and Connolly, Washington, D.C.

CHARLES HORNER, Senior Fellow, Hudson Institute, Washington, D.C.

KATHLEEN MARTINEZ, Executive Director, World Institute on Disability

GEORGE E. MOOSE, Adjunct Professor of Practice, The George Washington University, Washington, D.C.

JEREMY A. RABKIN, Professor of Law, George Mason University. Fairfax, Va.

Ron Silver, Actor, Producer, Director, Primparous Productions, Inc.

Judy Van Rest, Executive Vice President, International Republican Institute, Washington, D.C.

Members ex officio

Condoleezza Rice, Secretary of State

Robert M. Gates, Secretary of Defense

Richard H. Solomon, President, United States Institute of Peace (nonvoting)

Frances C. Wilson, Lieutenant General, U.S. Marine Corps; President, National Defense University

NEGOTIATING ARAB-ISRAELI PEACE
American Leadership in the Middle East

Text is set in Adobe Garamond
Cover Design: Kim Hasten Design Studio
Interior Design and Page Makeup: Cynthia Jordan
Developmental Editor: Brian Slattery
Proofreading: Maine Proofreading Services
Cartographer: Dan Rothem

Golan Heights